KU-742-905

BRAIN BOOSTING

Brain training puzzles & facts to keep your brain young

Michael Powell

Bath · New York · Cologne · Melbourne · Delhi
Hong Kong · Shenzhen · Singapore · Amsterdam

This edition published by Parragon Books Ltd in 2014

Parragon Books Ltd
Chartist House
15–17 Trim Street
Bath BA1 1HA, UK
www.parragon.com

Copyright © Parragon Books Ltd 2014

Arrangement copyright © Susanna Geoghegan
Illustrations pp 101, 102, 105 © Katy Jackson
Packaged by Susanna Geoghegan
Cover design by Talking Design
Inside designed by Angela Wilkinson

All rights reserved. No part of this publication may be reproduced, stored in a retrieval
system or transmitted, in any form or by any means, electronic, mechanical, photocopying,
recording or otherwise, without the prior permission of the copyright holder.

ISBN: 978-1-4723-6421-0

Printed in China

CONTENTS

INTRODUCTION

THE BRAIN IS THE CENTRE OF THE HUMAN NERVOUS SYSTEM, GOVERNING OUR THOUGHTS, FEELINGS AND MOVEMENTS; IT FILTERS AND PRIORITIZES ALL THE INFORMATION THAT BOMBARDS OUR SENSES EVEN WHILE WE SLEEP; IT CONTROLS OUR AUTONOMIC FUNCTIONS FROM SWALLOWING AND BREATHING TO HEART RATE AND PERSPIRATION; IT CONSTANTLY MODIFIES OUR MEMORIES TO IMPROVE OUR DECISION-MAKING ABILITIES AND FROM EARLY INFANCY IT ALLOWS US TO DEVELOP THE SELF-AWARENESS THAT MAKES US UNIQUELY HUMAN.

Life moulds your brain; since you were born it has been developing and fine-tuning the network of connections, the pattern of associations, stitching together the rich tapestry of genetic inheritance and life experience that has brought you to this moment, right here, right now, reading these words. You will respond to them as only you can because only your brain can occupy this precise point in space-time (although smarter human brains have formulated the theories that accommodate countless other yous in infinite parallel worlds within the multiverse).

Fortunately, brains are spectacularly plastic, meaning they continue to develop throughout our lives; the functional restructuring of brain cells means that it's never too late to learn new information, change your thought processes and boost your brain power. Recent research into gamma waves at the Kavli Institute for Systems Neuroscience and Centre for the Biology of Memory at the Norwegian University of Science and Technology (NTNU) has shown that signalling inside the brain isn't restricted to the modification of connections between neurons; the brain is even more flexible than that. These Norwegian scientists now believe that brain cells use a switching system to literally tune into each other's wavelengths; they receive thousands of inputs and they can choose which to ignore and which to listen to, by tuning into different gamma wavelengths, much like turning the dial on a radio.

Even our memories are more fluid than you might think; they are constantly being updated and changed to inform our current circumstances. Every time we re-activate a memory we reinforce and subtly change it, depending on our current interpretation. Bereavement is a good example of the fluidity of memory and how experiences can be viewed differently over time.

All this flexibility is fantastic news for those who recognize the importance of good brain health, stimulation and development. This book is a multigym for your mind. It's a brain fitness system made up of a wide range of puzzles, brain teasers, quizzes and challenges designed for performing different mental tasks to give you a focused workout. The target areas are concentration, problem-solving, language, numbers, visual perception, memory and creativity. Each topic introduces a compelling idea in the field of metacognition, followed by a selection of related questions and exercises – more than 200 of them.

It is well established that mental exercises during childhood and late adulthood contribute to a slower mental decline in old age, but did you know that a team at Tübingen University in Germany has proposed a theory that healthy old people don't suffer mental decline at all? They just know so much that their brains take longer to process all the information, in the same way that a computer's hard drive slows down when it's full.

You can read this book cover to cover or dip in and out as you please since most of the topics are self-contained, although some of them refer back to earlier sections. Say no to mental decline, read on and start to become more productive today!

CONCENTRATION AND FOCUS
SKILLS TEST

This quiz is designed to assess your concentration levels.

Strongly Agree	Agree	Neutral	Disagree	Strongly Disagree
1	2	3	4	5

1. My mind often wanders when I am trying to concentrate.

2. When concentrating I quickly become tired.

3. I rarely use strategies and motivational techniques to help me achieve boring or challenging tasks.

4. Other people always seem to be disturbing me.

5. When I most need to concentrate is when I feel most distracted.

6. I don't know which times of day are my most productive so I don't arrange my schedule to tackle difficult tasks at optimum times.

7. I try to do several things at once and flit between them.

8. I don't set goals and objectives before starting a project.

9. I regularly check social media while I'm working.

10. I repeat the same things over and over again because I lose track.

11. I can't concentrate if someone is chatting nearby.

12. I feel rushed.

13. I get bored easily.

14. I push on through tasks and rarely take short breaks.

15. My working environment is not conducive to concentration.

16. The task takes as long as it takes, so I don't set time goals.

17. I always feel like the fun is happening somewhere else and I'm missing it.

18. I often forget what I am supposed to be doing or what comes next.

19. I can only stay focused on something if it's really interesting.

20. I suffer from intrusive thoughts.

21. This quiz is boring.

22. My study area is tidy and uncluttered.

23. I rarely work in a place free from auditory and visual distractions.

24. I fidget and/or find it hard to sit still.

25. I procrastinate.

Total score:

RESULTS

25–50

You are in urgent need of some strategies to aid your concentration. You may have problems beginning tasks and may suffer from anxiety as a result of your lack of focus. You tire easily, are easily distracted and never seem to have enough time to complete your work. You have a low boredom threshold and often blame others for your inability to concentrate.

51–75

You sometimes use strategies to aid your concentration but would benefit from setting goals, structuring your work environment and setting time limits to increase your focus. You should also take short breaks when your attention wanders. You take some responsibility for your own concentration but still prefer gossiping around the water cooler to getting your head down for some full-on focused work.

76–100

On the whole you enjoy good concentration and usually take full responsibility for structuring your work environment and minimizing distractions. However, you still have moments when you go into meltdown and just can't seem to focus, which means you would benefit from taking breaks and using some of the techniques in this chapter to give you extra motivation when your energy is flagging.

101–125

Your mind is laser sharp and your focus and self-discipline are in the top percentile. You have a wealth of strategies and inner resources to draw upon when the going gets tough. You can stick to even the most thankless tasks because you set clear goals, use your time efficiently and always take full responsibility for structuring your work environment and minimizing distractions.

INCREASE PRODUCTIVITY

Staying focused can be a big challenge and isn't always about working harder or blitzing a problem with extra resources. Software developers are familiar with Brooks's law which states that 'adding manpower to a late software project makes it later'. Increasing productivity involves acting smarter to maximize your cognitive assets: you can't change the number of hours in the day but you can transform the way you use them.

1. Scientific studies have linked ambient temperature to productivity and show that the 'comfort zone' is between 22°C/72°F and 25°C/77°F.

2. Make a plan for the day. Set ambitious but realistic goals. If your goals are overambitious you are setting yourself up to fail and destroying your future motivation.

3. Now just start and your fears of failure/lack of time will greatly reduce. If a huge project overwhelms you, break it down into manageable chunks.

4. Trust in the competence and sincerity of others. Ask for help when you need it and share your expertise with others in return.

5. Less is more. Productivity is not measured by how long you sit at your desk. Work in short bursts with maximum focus and take short breaks when your attention wanders.

6. Tell other people about your goals so that you feel more accountable for them.

7. Find your most productive time of day and start work then, even if it is 5 am or 11 pm. If it feels right to you, don't worry about conforming with the nine-to-fivers.

8. Change your environment. Sometimes just moving into another room and working with paper and pen instead of a computer can re-motivate you and promote creativity.

9. Follow the Pareto principle (devised by Italian economist Vilfredo Pareto and also known as the 80–20 rule), which states that for many events, 80 per cent of the effects come from 20 per cent of the causes. What 20 per cent of fruitless activities are wasting 80 per cent of your time?

10. Focus on one thing at a time. Research has shown that multitasking is inefficient.

Less is more: the solutions to these puzzles are easier and require less work than you might think.

BARREL OF BEER

Is the barrel of beer more than half full or less than half full?
There is a way you can tell without using any additional equipment.

THREE LIGHT BULBS

The three switches on the wall outside the windowless room are connected to three bulbs inside the room. How can you work out which switch is connected to which bulb if you are only allowed to enter the room once?

GOOD SAMARITAN

The Pareto principle is the idea that in many systems there is inequality between causes and effects. In this puzzle, one choice you make is vital while the others only offer small returns.

You are driving down the road in your car on a wild, stormy night,
when you pass by a bus stop and you see three people waiting for the bus:

1. An old lady who looks like she is about to die.

2. An old friend who once saved your life.

3. The perfect partner of your dreams.

You can only fit one passenger in your car. Who should you choose?

ATTENTIONAL CONTROL

Attention and focus are critical skills that help us to absorb, process and memorize information. Attentional control (AC) is the capacity to choose what to pay attention to and what to ignore, how effectively we can engage and disengage our focus. In many ways it defines who we are. The Spanish philosopher José Ortega y Gasset said, 'Tell me to what you pay attention, and I will tell you who you are.'

AC primarily involves the frontal areas of the brain including the anterior cingulate cortex and it is closely related to working memory. It is greater in adults than children because their frontal lobes are still developing, but even in adulthood you can greatly improve this crucial cognitive skill. Disrupted AC is related to conditions such as Attention Deficit Hyperactivity Disorder (ADHD) and autism.

It is also adversely affected by anxiety but impaired AC has been identified as one of the primary cognitive factors underlying the origin and maintenance of anxiety. In other words, reducing your anxiety will improve your AC, but also improving your AC and focusing on the task at hand will reduce your anxiety.

The best way to improve your AC is by practice: performing tasks with the prime motivation of refusing to allow yourself to become distracted. However, setting up your environment and mindset is also key. Remember, research has shown that self-discipline is more important than IQ in predicting academic success:

1. Eliminate distractions: turn off TV and music and remove devices such as your mobile phone. Simplify your visual field (e.g. when doing desk work, remove post-it notes and all other clutter from your desk).

2. Work in manageable chunks of time: 15–45 minutes with a short break in between.

3. Understand WHY you are doing the task and how it will benefit you or others.

4. Set a clear goal so you understand WHAT you are doing and monitor your behaviour towards that goal.

5. Break tasks down into components, so you don't become overwhelmed and demotivated by the size of the whole task. Work on one task at a time.

MIXED SIGNALS

This exercise involves blocking out one or more stimuli to focus exclusively on another. Many people are already very skilled at this when they so choose (we all have friends and family who won't acknowledge our existence while they watch television, play video games or text).

Pick one or more competing stimuli (aural, tactile, visual, olfactory, taste), e.g.: blaring television/radio, lights flashing on and off (get a friend to help), sucking a lemon, being bashed on the head at random intervals by a balloon, sitting in a cold bath, etc. Now tune a second radio onto a speaking station. During a five-minute period, count the number of times the speakers say the word 'the'. Notice how the 'game' aspect reduces the negative emotional component (i.e. irritation).

COUNT THE SQUARES

How many squares are there in this picture?
92 per cent of people fail this simple attention test!

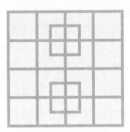

HOW MANY Fs?

How many Fs are there in each of these sentences? Read them only once and write down your answers within sixty seconds.

1. Finished files are the result of years of scientific study combined with the experience of years.

2. For a strange definition of fun, consider that all that fun means is that four out of five people enjoy counting Fs.

3. It is easy to miss the finer points in life; folk are frequently guilty of falling into this trap.

HOW TO DEAL WITH
INTRUSIVE THOUGHTS

Intrusive thoughts are almost always created by anxiety and/or negative emotional experiences. They hinder your concentration, encourage you to procrastinate, distract you from the task in hand and inevitably increase your anxiety, which can lead to an increase in intrusive thoughts.

Trying to block out unwanted thoughts is actually counterproductive. Close your eyes right now and set a timer. Your aim is to spend a minute without thinking of a white bear.

How did you get on? How many seconds did you last before the white bear appeared in your thoughts? And why do we think of a white bear when we have expressly told ourselves not to?

Daniel Wegner, a psychology professor at Harvard University, pioneer in the field of thought suppression and author of *White Bears and Other Unwanted Thoughts*, has shown that trying to suppress thought leads to obsession.

So, don't block out unwanted thoughts or earworms (the name given to snippets of a catchy song playing on a loop in your head). Instead, congratulate yourself for recognizing that you are experiencing them and realizing that your concentration is wandering.

Wegner offers several strategies to deal with your white bears:

1. Focus on something else instead! If you are cognitively engaged, it limits the ability of intrusive thoughts to enter your head.

2. Try to postpone the thought. Write a list of the things that are bothering you and then set it aside to be dealt with at an assigned point later in the day. This means that you don't have to hold the thoughts in your memory and you know that you will deal with them later.

3. Wherever possible, avoid multitasking, which can reduce productivity by approximately 40 per cent according to some researchers, as well as increasing stress and anxiety.

4. Exposure: 'This is painful,' Wegner said, 'but it can work.' Allow yourself to think about the unwanted thought, so that it is less likely to pop up unwanted at other times.

5. Meditation and mindfulness strengthen mental control and help to control unwanted thoughts.

REMOVE EARWORMS

Dr Ira Hyman, a music psychologist at Western Washington University, claims the best way to stop earworms is to solve some tricky anagrams.

FINE IN TORN JEANS	American actress (F)
NARCOLEPTIC	English musician (M)
CRAZED I MOAN	American actress (F)
ERROR ON BIDET	American actor (M)
ELITE BRAIN NEST	Theoretical physicist (M)
I DEMAND TV LATER	American television host (M)
A FAMOUS GERMAN WALTZ GOD	Composer of the Classical era (M)
MORMON IDEAS	American singer (F)
I RULE STAR JOB	American actress (F)
HE'S GROWN LARGE N CRAZED	American actor turned politician (M)
LEAN WAR MISSILE	Tennis champion (F)
USE MY LYRIC	American actress and recording artist (F)

OBJECT FOCUS

Take a small simple object such as a glass or a piece of fruit. Concentrate on and explore it. Turn it over in your hands to experience the object without using thoughts. See if you can shift all your focus onto the object with a quiet, non-judgemental mind.

CLOCK WATCH

This exercise was suggested by Vanda North and Richard Israel, the authors of *Mind Chi*. Focus on the second hand of a clock on the wall, while repeating the word 'one' until a stray thought pops into your mind. Then say 'two' over and over until you spot the next thought, and then start saying 'three'. See how low you can keep your score during a one-minute clock watch.

AWAKEN YOUR SENSES

It is all too easy to neglect our five senses and miss out on a plethora of fun ways to boost brain performance. Stimulating taste, touch, smell, hearing and vision directly before applying yourself to a specific task can improve concentration and alertness.

SIGHT

Research at the University of Hiroshima in Japan has found that looking at pictures of cute animals improves concentration. Tests on 132 university students showed they performed better in cognitive tests after looking at photos of baby animals, but not after viewing their adult counterparts. Students who viewed cute animals improved their performance in an Operation-style game (which tests hand–eye coordination and fine motor skills) by 44 per cent. The researchers concluded, 'Cute images are considered to induce positive affect with high approach motivation because they are evolutionarily related to caregiving and nurturing or because they prime social engagement.'

Exposure to colour has an important effect on moods and feelings, which impact concentration. Green is considered to be the colour of concentration. If you haven't already painted your study area green, place some green objects on your desk and reserve a particular favourite article of green clothing to wear only when you need to concentrate. Best of all, spend ten minutes walking in nature before you start work.

SMELL

Several studies have shown that peppermint aroma improves memory, focus and concentration. In one study in Cincinnati, Ohio, a group of students who were exposed to the aroma of peppermint oil before a test showed an improved accuracy of 28 per cent.

Lemon balm can also boost memory and mood. Its cognitive benefits have been extolled for centuries. In the sixteenth century, herbalist John Gerard offered it to his students to 'quicken the senses'. Laboratory tests on this common weed have found it increases the activity of acetylcholine, a chemical messenger linked to memory.

Other scents that aid concentration include jasmine, cinnamon, vanilla, vetiver, cedarwood and rosemary (which increases blood flow to the head and brain). Care should be taken when using essential oils to provide these scents.

TASTE

Instead of reaching for your customary cup of coffee, suck on a lemon or sip a glass of iced lemon or lime juice, which will hydrate you while the sourness increases your alertness.

Research published in the journal *Psychological Science* by scientists at the University of Georgia indicates that just the taste of sugar (gargling with lemonade made from real sugar) improved the focus and self-control of test subjects. Co-author Leonard Martin explains: 'After this trial, it seems that glucose stimulates the simple carbohydrates sensors on your tongue,' which 'signals the motivation centres of the brain'.

TOUCH

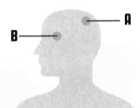

Several acupressure points improve memory and concentration, relieve headaches and aid relaxation. Self-massage or apply gentle fingertip pressure at these points.

(A) One Hundred Meeting Point (on the crown of the head in between the cranial bones)

(B) Sun Point (in the depression of the temples)

(C) Gates of Consciousness (the hollows below the base of the skull)

(D) Heavenly Pillar (half an inch below the base of the skull on muscles one-half inch either side of the spine)

(E) Three Mile Point (four finger widths below the kneecap, one finger width outside of the shinbone)

(F) Bigger Rushing (in the dimple between the big toe and the second toe)

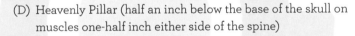

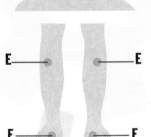

HEARING

Binaural beats are an intriguing way to change your brain waves to aid concentration (or send you to sleep, depending on your requirements). They involve playing tones of slightly differing frequencies into each ear via stereo headphones before or even while you work. Search YouTube for 'binaural beats concentration'.

DIGITAL DISTRACTIONS

It is a fact of life that most of us are becoming increasingly reliant on technology from smart phones to the internet, but while technology and social media have many benefits, research psychologists such as Dr Larry Rosen believe that our overuse of smart phones, tablets and computers is creating widespread mental health issues.

In his book *iDisorder: Understanding Our Obsession with Technology and Overcoming Its Hold on Us*, Rosen warns that 'many of us are on the verge of an iDisorder' caused by 'the way we all relate to technology and media' which expresses the symptoms of several psychological disorders, 'including narcissism, obsessive-compulsive disorder, depression, attention-deficit disorder, social phobia, antisocial personality disorder, hypochondriasis, body dysmorphic disorder, schizo-disorders and voyeurism'. If you are 'plugged in' you may already recognize unhealthy aspects of your own relationship with technology: wasting an hour online when you only intended to send an email; checking your text messages during the middle of the night; mentally rehearsing a twitter update instead of experiencing the moment.

Do you have an iDisorder?

If you can answer yes to five or more of these questions, you may have a problem:

1. Do you feel anxious that you're missing out if you can't regularly check your emails/social media?

2. Do you lie in bed checking your phone/tablet before you go to sleep?

3. Do you often bring your laptop when you sit on the toilet?

4. Do you refresh your inbox over and over in case someone emailed you in the last 30 seconds?

5. Do you change your Facebook profile picture more than twice in a month?

6. Do you say things online that you wouldn't dream of saying to someone's face?

7. Do you regularly think your phone is vibrating in your pocket even when it isn't?

8. Do you interrupt tasks in order to check your emails/social media?

9. Do you use your mobile phone while driving (not hands free)?

10. Do you tweet/post on social media in the middle of the night to announce that you can't sleep?

Studies show that students who checked Facebook just once during a 15-minute study period performed worse. Constantly checking our devices becomes an obsessive feedback loop, often driven by what MTV called FOMO (*fear of missing out*) and Dr Jim Taylor from the University of San Francisco calls DA (*disconnectivity anxiety*).

The anxiety experienced when those technologies are not available (having to switch off a smart phone in a cinema, the internet goes down), the disruption to sleep caused by interacting with technology before bedtime, not to mention the narcissistic obsession with how one presents oneself online, all add up to iDisorder.

So how do we maintain focus when technology and social media constantly threaten to distract us? Here are three ways to reduce your dependence on technology:

SPEND MORE TIME WITH NATURE

Spending even a few minutes interacting with a natural environment helps to calm and reset the brain and improve its ability to function. Scientists at the University of Michigan have even discovered that ten minutes spent looking at photographs of nature offers the same restorative effects as the real thing.

LISTEN TO MUSIC

Dr Larry Rosen says, 'music activates the same reward circuits in the brain that react to food and sex, and brain scans have shown that just listening to music for a short time can help reset the brain'.

RETHINK, REBOOT, RECONNECT AND REVITALIZE

Science and technology journalist Daniel Sieberg's four-step plan encourages you to:

Rethink: work out how much time you spend interacting with technology.
Reboot: disconnect for a period to break your habitual behaviours.
Reconnect: gradually reintroduce technology, but now with a greater awareness; restructure your environment so that you control the technology (e.g. place your tablet/mobile phone in another room while you focus exclusively on an important task without interruption).
Revitalize: prioritize human contact.

THE 'FIVE MORE' RULE

HOW MUCH WILLPOWER DO YOU HAVE?

1. When I am performing a difficult task I
    a) try to finish as quickly as possible so that I can put my feet up
    b) enjoy the challenge
    c) worry that I won't be able to complete it/lose my temper/pay someone else to do it

2. When trying to stick to a new regime (diet, work schedule, financial budget) I
    a) stick rigidly to the rules
    b) allow myself the occasional lapse without beating myself up about it
    c) quickly cave in to temptation/quit after a few days

3. Other people seem to have it easier than me
    a) sometimes
    b) rarely
    c) always

4. I keep promises I make to myself
    a) sometimes
    b) always
    c) rarely

5. Hard work pays off
    a) sometimes
    b) always
    c) rarely

6. The most useful question I can ask is
    a) why?
    b) why not?
    c) why me?

7. When something isn't working out I
    a) keep plugging away
    b) review the situation and I'm not afraid to change direction if required
    c) get stressed out/give up/blame someone else

8. I would best describe willpower as:
    a) a finite resource that runs out and needs refilling (e.g. a water butt)
    b) a self-renewing supply that always gives as much as I require (an underground lake)
    c) something only other people seem to possess

RESULTS

Mostly As

You have some willpower but it's all or nothing with you. Sometimes you aren't prepared to put in the consistent work to get the results that you desire and shirk responsibility for your failures. You have a tendency to think something or someone else is responsible for your problems and their solutions.

Mostly Bs

You have the traits of a highly successful person, combining willpower and consistency with the ability to admit your own failings. You have the confidence and flexibility to change tack when a new strategy is required. You take pleasure in being creative and seeing where opportunities can take you, without being too much of a perfectionist.

Mostly Cs

You need to learn to take responsibility for your future by getting busy in the present moment. You lack self-reliance because your previous setbacks have dented your motivation and spirit of adventure. The good news is that you can improve your prospects instantly by asking a little bit more from yourself with the 'five more' rule.

When you feel your attention wandering or you want to quit, just do FIVE MORE – stay on task for five more minutes, read five more pages, do five more reps in the gym, do five more maths problems.

It is important to recognize that the prevailing belief that willpower is a finite reserve is actually untrue and unhelpful. It is not a well that runs dry (unless you believe that it is). Stanford University psychology professors Greg Walton and Carol Dweck followed 153 college students over five weeks and found that students who had been taught that willpower was unlimited and self-renewing exhibited increases in willpower and reported eating less junk food and procrastinating less than students who had been taught that willpower was finite. Subsequently they also earned better grades.

Walton and Dweck's explanation is that 'People who think that willpower is limited are on the lookout for signs of fatigue. When they detect fatigue, they slack off' whereas people who are taught that willpower is unlimited learn to view fatigue not as a reason to quit, but 'a sign to dig deeper and find more resources'. So the more you follow the five more rule, the easier you will find it to follow the five more rule! You can push beyond what you thought biologically and mentally possible by incrementally increasing your commitment and stamina.

IMPROVE YOUR
REACTION TIME

Although reactions decrease with age, they are a consistent indicator of general fitness, health and how well you are taking care of yourself. The best ways to improve your reaction time are to get adequate sleep, eat healthily, take plenty of exercise and avoid drugs and alcohol.

Your reactions change throughout the day, so you can use these two tests to gauge when you are at your most productive. Also, keeping track of your reaction time over several weeks can be a big motivator if you are trying to improve your mental and physical fitness.

One of the best ways to improve your reaction time is to relax. Using your imagination to 'go through the motions' – visualizing the physical movements that your body needs to perform for a given task – has also been shown to speed up reaction times in real-life situations. Sports people spend a lot of time training their muscle memory to increase their speed and accuracy.

Sugar and high glycaemic foods can cause drowsiness and slow down reactions, while a little shot of caffeine will boost your performance (although overdo the coffee and it will quickly decline). If you need an energy boost, avoid sugary foods and drinks and chew a stick of gum instead. A team of scientists at Japan's Chiba University found that students improved their reaction times by seven per cent by chewing gum. This may be because the jaw muscles stimulate areas of the brain, including the premotor cortex within the frontal lobe, which is involved in preparing and executing limb movements.

LEFT RIGHT UP DOWN

1. Working from left to right, top to bottom, call out the direction that the eyes are looking (from your perspective). Time yourself. Keep practising until you can do it in only 15 seconds.

2. Now add a layer of complexity by calling out the direction from the face's perspective.

3. Finally, call out the opposite direction (from your perspective, or if you are a real masochist, from the face's). This is the ultimate challenge but that feeling you are tying yourself in knots works wonders inside your brain.

BALL DROP

A helper holds a football out to the side of their body at shoulder height. When s/he drops the ball, you must sprint to catch it before it bounces for a second time. Vary the sprinting distance according to your ability so the drill is challenging without being impossible.

IMPROVE YOUR BRAIN'S
PROCESSING SPEED

Brain processing speed is how fast your brain can process information and perform cognitive functions over time and it is one of the ways that intelligence is measured. Your brain has about 100 billion cells called neurons which receive and transmit electrochemical signals. Each neuron contains branched projections called dendrites which receive electrochemical messages from other neurons, which then travel through a cable-like structure in the cell called an axon before jumping to other neurons across junctions called synapses.

The brain needs optimum nutrients and daily training to attain maximum performance. Physical exercise and healthy dietary choices are the best ways to improve cognitive speed. Exercise stimulates blood circulation, increases blood flow to the brain and stimulates hormones that are responsible for cell repair and generation. The best physical exercise, such as sports and dancing, engages your mind as well as your body and requires advanced coordination.

The neural axons are protected and insulated by a material called myelin (which looks like a string of sausages). The myelin increases the speed at which impulses are transmitted (impaired myelin is present in many neurodegenerative diseases such as multiple sclerosis and Guillain–Barré syndrome). Myelin sheath function declines with age, which is one of the reasons that processing speed also declines with age. But, according to the clinical nutritionist Byron Richards, three dietary supplements may provide nutritional support for myelin sheathing: Calcium AEP (amino ethanol phosphate), Phosphatidylserine (also present in soy lecithin, Atlantic herring, chicken heart, offal) and fat-soluble antioxidants, such as the tocotrienol form of vitamin E (also present in low levels in select rice bran oil, palm oil, wheatgerm and barley).

Games with time limits are excellent brain-speed boosters because they force you to perform an activity within a set time. For brain-speed training, choose puzzles and games where the goal is speed and accuracy rather than open-ended puzzles where simply solving the problem is the main focus. Rhythm games are also useful because they force you to make decisions quickly. Just as lifting heavy weights builds muscle strength, doing daily brain exercises where speed is essential increases brain speed.

SAY MY NAME

Time yourself to see how quickly you can:

a) say the number of letters of the word (five, four, five . . .)

b) add consecutive numbers horizontally (eight, twelve, seventeen, eighteen . . .)

c) add consecutive numbers vertically (ten, sixteen, eleven, ten . . .)

3	5	7	10	8	5	10	3	4	10
7	10	8	2	3	4	10	5	10	8
9	8	10	2	10	10	2	6	3	7
2	1	9	1	5	1	3	9	5	5
8	1	2	3	2	7	1	9	8	4
9	5	9	7	7	2	7	9	7	1
10	9	5	1	4	5	8	7	5	1
4	5	1	9	8	3	7	6	8	10
5	5	1	7	1	6	9	6	2	2
7	3	8	9	10	9	6	6	3	10

SLAP, CLAP, SNAP, SNAP

Establish a slow rhythm by slapping your legs with both hands once (slap), clapping once (clap) and then clicking right and left fingers in turn (snap, snap).

Pick a topic (animals, cars, flowers, etc.). When you slap your legs, call out an example of your chosen topic that begins with the letter 'A', then on the next leg slap, one that begins with 'B' and so on. Slow down the rhythm so you can get through the alphabet without stopping. If you falter, keep the rhythm going and resume on the leg slap. You may repeat a topic and speed up the rhythm to test your memory and challenge your brain to process more quickly.

COLOUR MATCH 'SNAP'

Playing on your own (or with another player) and using a standard 52-card deck, deal cards face up one by one (so that each card covers the next) and shout out 'snap' whenever the current card matches the colour of the previous one (i.e. both red or both black).

SOLUTION-FOCUSED
THINKING

Understand the problem, then focus everything on the solution. It sounds easy, but many of us just focus on the problem, are often overwhelmed and filled with anxiety by its negative consequences and end up procrastinating. Others dive into the solution without fully understanding or addressing the problem. This risks seeking a solution to the wrong problem or a problem that doesn't even exist.

UNDERSTAND THE PROBLEM

Successful companies look at what their customers need – their problems – and try to solve them with their products. Unsuccessful companies design solutions for the wrong problems or problems which don't even exist, or they launch products that don't fill a need. A new product flops when its designers focus on the solution without considering the problem.

In the seventies, a leading brand of shampoo famously bombed because its unique selling point – that it contained yogurt – just didn't wash with its customers. The high-profile launch of a ready-to-drink coffee product also tanked because it promised convenience (just pop in the microwave) but the solution didn't solve the problem (if pouring boiling water on coffee beans/ granules was ever a problem in the first place) because the carton itself could not be heated in the microwave.

Apple's global success has been based on making a few products really well, rather than lots of products less well. Apple identifies a need/problem and then designs a simple paradigm-shifting solution that blows the competition out of the water. Its solutions have been so appropriate that Apple sometimes appears to invent things we couldn't have imagined and didn't even know we needed.

One of the most vital considerations at the problem-understanding stage is to examine your assumptions about the problem. This is especially important when you are working in a group: conflicting assumptions will always scupper a solution because they indicate a failure to understand and agree on the problem.

FOCUS ON THE SOLUTION

Your mind works best when it is directed on one thing. You can either move in the direction of the problem or the solution but not both at the same time. Once you've understood the problem it is time to change direction towards the solution, because as we all know, problems grow bigger when we brood on them.

No one understands this better than Dr Aaron Beck, the father of Cognitive-Behavioural Therapy and co-founder of the Beck Institute. He discovered that 'every disorder has some degree of self-focus' and that focusing on the problem inevitably makes it worse. He has helped many social anxiety sufferers to take their focus away from themselves so that they can socially engage and counter the self-reinforcing belief that was perpetuating their social isolation. He observes that people suffering from chronic pain experience a reduction in pain when their focus is directed towards something else: 'get them into a conversation . . . they are no longer grimacing . . . the pain is greatly diminished . . . their emotional or psychological investment for the time being has been diminished'. The long-term solution is to set new goals and focus on these precisely because the goals are the solution.

Focusing on the solution lights a fire under you and drives you into a decisive action; focusing on the problem leads to inactivity and paralysing fear. Problems rarely solve themselves; they are usually resolved by action.

ARE YOU PROBLEM-ORIENTED OR SOLUTION-ORIENTED?

1. When I look at problems, situations and people, I work from the assumption that
   a) many people can't be trusted
   b) the vast majority of people are basically good and trustworthy
   c) the relationships and connections I make are more important than finding a solution

2. All problems can be solved if we have the will
   a) I strongly disagree
   b) I strongly agree
   c) it depends on the problem

3. When faced with a new challenge I feel

   a) anxious

   b) excited

   c) both

4. When I have to perform an unpleasant but necessary chore I

   a) think about all the reasons why I hate it and ways I can avoid doing it

   b) get straight on and do it, so I can focus on doing something else that I do enjoy

   c) have a moan, put it off as long as possible, then find it's not as bad as I thought it would be

5. When I have to perform an unfamiliar task I

   a) spend so much time feeling worried and unprepared that when I do begin I feel rushed

   b) focus on completing the task to the best of my ability after a short preparation

   c) usually only feel ready to begin after considerable preparation

6. I evaluate the usefulness or non-usefulness of a task

   a) before, during and after

   b) before

   c) rarely

7. I begin tasks without knowing why I am doing them

   a) always

   b) never

   c) sometimes

8. I have more than my fair share of problems

   a) strongly agree

   b) strongly disagree

   c) sometimes

RESULTS

Mostly As

You are highly problem-oriented. Life frequently feels like a succession of obstacles and inconveniences, often caused by other people. You regularly firefight instead of planning ahead. Sometimes you experience high levels of doubt and anxiety which prevent you from beginning and completing projects and you often feel rushed. You rarely focus fully on a solution because you are distracted by the problem, ways to avoid it and doubts about the usefulness of the task.

Mostly Bs

You are highly solution-oriented. You like and trust others and see problems as opportunities. You understand the importance of good preparation but you recognize that results are more important than the process. You establish the importance of a task at the outset, so your motivation to complete it isn't hampered by doubts. You set clear goals and believe that you can achieve them.

Mostly Cs

You are a conscientious and fairly positive person but you experience bouts of self-doubt and procrastination. You can enjoy a challenge but sometimes you invest a little too much energy into preparation and reading around the subject, and rarely feel quite ready enough to tackle a new situation. When you finally start a project you have a tendency to enjoy the process more than finding a solution.

DIGITAL DILEMMA

You have fifteen minutes to find a solution to this problem. While you work, try to be aware of the thoughts, positive and negative, that pop into your head and HOW you approach the problem, with respect to the issues raised in the questionnaire about being solution-oriented, anxiety levels, your motivation or lack of it and your ability to stay focused on the solution rather than being distracted by the usefulness of the task.

How can you use all the ascending consecutive digits 1, 2, 3, 4, 5, 6, 7, 8, 9, combined with any combination of just six plus or minus signs to reach the total 100? (e.g. 1 + 23 - 4 + 5 . . .)

___ +/- ___ +/- ___ +/- ___ +/- ___ +/- ___ +/- ___ = 100

LOGICAL REASONING

IN ITS SIMPLEST DEFINITION, LOGICAL
REASONING INVOLVES COMBINING A SET
OF PREMISES TO REACH A LOGICALLY VALID
CONCLUSION. IF THE PREMISES ARE TRUE, THEN
THE CONCLUSION MUST ALSO BE TRUE.

Logic was studied and developed in many ancient civilizations, including India, China and Persia, but the greatest influence on Western thought has been Aristotle, the ancient Greek philosopher, born in 384 BC, who is credited with inventing the formal discipline of logic.

Aristotle's followers (the Peripatetics) grouped together six of Aristotle's treatises under the title *Organon (Instrument)*, which formed the basis of the earliest formal study of logic until the collapse of the Roman Empire 800 years later.

Islamic and Jewish scholars continued to translate and study the Greek texts during the Early Middle Ages, but most of Aristotle's logical works had to wait until the twelfth century to be translated into Latin (a revival known as the 'Recovery of Aristotle'). Christian scholars such as Albertus Magnus and Thomas Aquinas then began to assimilate Aristotle's teaching into Christian theology, so by the sixteenth century his work had become intricately bound up with the Catholic Church, as sacred and untouchable as the Bible; anyone who challenged the authority of his teachings was persecuted as a heretic. The heresy of the Italian astronomer Galileo included the rejection of Aristotle's dynamics concerning the arrangement and movement of heavenly bodies and the notion of the heavens as a perfect, unchanging substance.

The Scientific Revolution and the Enlightenment challenged the authority of Aristotle and the Church in favour of reason and the advancement of knowledge through the scientific method. Despite this, Aristotle's logic remained the dominant form in the West until nineteenth-century advances in mathematical logic (most notably, the propositional calculus invented by the English mathematician George Boole – *see* page 40).

Logic is often broadly divided into three types: deductive reasoning, inductive reasoning and abductive reasoning.

DEDUCTIVE REASONING

The basis of Aristotle's deductive argument was the syllogism, which has three parts: major premise, minor premise and conclusion. For example,

> Premise 1: All A = B
> Premise 2: All C = A
> Conclusion: C = B

> Major premise: All humans are mortal.
> Minor premise: All Greeks are humans.
> Conclusion: All Greeks are mortal.

> Premise 1: No reptiles have fur.
> Premise 2: All snakes are reptiles.
> Conclusion: No snakes have fur.

In *Organon*, Aristotle gives the following definition: 'A syllogism is discourse in which certain things being stated, something other than what is stated follows of necessity from their being so. I mean by the last phrase that they produce a consequence, and by this, that no further term is required from without in order to make the consequence necessary.'

In syllogistic logic, there are 256 possible ways to construct categorical syllogisms but only 24 of them can be described as 'valid' (conclusion necessarily follows from the premises) and 19 of these are valid and 'unweakened' (it is not possible to strengthen them by the substitution of a particular sentence [some] for a universal one [all] in the conclusion).

In all valid syllogisms, at least one of the two premises must contain a universal form (i.e. using the word 'all'). If both premises are particulars (using the word 'some'), then no valid conclusion can result from them. Also, at least one of the two premises must be affirmative.

> Premise 1: Some dogs are dangerous.
> Premise 2: Some dangerous things are volcanoes.

It does not follow that 'some dogs are volcanoes' (because both premises are particulars).

However, a syllogism can still be logically valid without being true. For example, the conclusion in the following syllogism is logically valid and internally consistent, but untrue because it contains a 'false premise' (since unicorns don't exist).

Premise 1: All unicorns are animals.

Premise 2: Some unicorns are invisible.

Conclusion: Some animals are invisible.

Try these syllogisms out for size (follow the logic, not the truth). Here is one example of each of the 19 valid and unweakened modes of the classical syllogism:

Barbara

Premise 1: All birds have beaks.

Premise 2: All penguins are birds.

Conclusion: _____

Celarent

Premise 1: No birds have teeth.

Premise 2: All penguins are birds.

Conclusion: _____

Darii

Premise 1: All birds have feathers.

Premise 2: Some pets are birds.

Conclusion: _____

Ferio

Premise 1: No birds are dogs.

Premise 2: Some animals are birds.

Conclusion: _____

Cesare

Premise 1: No horse is a building.

Premise 2: All hotels are buildings.

Conclusion: _____

Camestres

Premise 1: All horses have hooves.

Premise 2: No carrots have hooves.

Conclusion: _____

Festino

Premise 1: No bald people are fat.

Premise 2: Some women are fat.

Conclusion: _____

Baroco

Premise 1: All carrots are vegetables.

Premise 2: Some pink things are not vegetables.

Conclusion: _____

Darapti

Premise 1: All fruit is nutritious.

Premise 2: All fruit is tasty.

Conclusion: _____

Disamis

Premise 1: Some butterflies are colourful.

Premise 2: All butterflies are delicate.

Conclusion: _____

Datisi

Premise 1: All gorillas are agile.

Premise 2: Some gorillas are endangered.

Conclusion: _____

Felapton

Premise 1: No fruit in this bowl is fresh.

Premise 2: All fruit in this bowl is yellow.

Conclusion: _____

Bocardo

Premise 1: Some cats have no tails.

Premise 2: All cats are animals.

Conclusion: _____

Ferison

Premise 1: No snakes have wheels.

Premise 2: Some snakes are green.

Conclusion: _____

Bramantip

Premise 1: All the socks in my wardrobe are purple.

Premise 2: All purple clothing is ostentatious.

Conclusion: _____

Camenes

Premise 1: All coloured flowers are scented.

Premise 2: No scented flowers are grown indoors.

Conclusion: _____

Dimaris

Premise 1: Some big dogs like cheese.

Premise 2: All dogs that like cheese are friendly.

Conclusion: _____

Fesapo

Premise 1: No Hollywood actors are happy.

Premise 2: All happy people are neighbourly.

Conclusion: _____

Fresison

Premise 1: No humans are pandas.

Premise 2: Some humans are evil.

Conclusion: _____

INDUCTIVE REASONING

Inductive reasoning involves deriving the general from the particular. It is the direct inverse of deduction, which involves deriving the particular from the general. Inductive reasoning requires guesswork to observe patterns in specific data, formulate a generalization from them and then test this hypothesis to reach the most credible conclusion.

Unlike deductive reasoning, inductive reasoning provides a conclusion that is neither watertight nor inevitable, merely the most credible. Inductive reasoning relies on one or more premises that are generalizations rather than absolutes, so the conclusions merely give a strong indication of the truth rather than absolute certainty. There is always a possibility that the conclusion is false.

Statistical syllogisms are examples of inductive reasoning.

Premise 1: *Almost all A are B.*
Premise 2: *C is A.*
Conclusion: *Therefore C is almost certainly B.*

Premise 1: *Almost all birds can fly.*
Premise 2: *An eagle is a bird.*
Conclusion: *Therefore an eagle can almost certainly fly.*

Pick a breed of bird at random to replace eagle and you stand a good chance of your conclusion being correct. However, there are about 40 species of flightless birds in existence today (e.g. penguin, ostrich) and all baby birds are initially flightless, so even an eagle cannot be said with complete certainty to fly.

Inductive reasoning has been criticized by many logicians and philosophers. Philosophical Skepticism argues that nothing can be absolute or true with unconditional certainty because all human experience is subjective and incomplete. However, Immanuel Kant argued in his masterpiece *The Critique of Pure Reason* that this is precisely the reason why we must rely on both inductive and deductive reasoning, in his famous statement: 'thoughts without content are empty, intuitions without concepts are blind'. In other words, our subjective understanding of the external world is founded on experience (inductive reasoning) and *a priori* concepts (deductive reasoning).

Inductive reasoning is necessary because we don't know all the fundamental laws of nature so we have to guess and formulate generalizations from observation and then test them – this is the basis of the modern scientific method.

If all this philosophy is making your head spin, you can at least thank inductive reasoning for helping us all to stay sane! For example, we inductively reason that the sun will rise tomorrow because that's what it has done for every previous day of our lives and back through written history. When you take a flight in an aeroplane you invariably use inductive reasoning to reassure yourself that you will survive the flight, although you can't be 100 per cent sure.

Premise 1:   *The vast majority of plane flights do not result in a crash.*
Premise 2:   *This is a plane flight.*
Conclusion: *It almost certainly will not result in a crash.*

Your plane NOT crashing is the pattern that best fits the observable data. How comforting!

INDUCTIVE REASONING TESTS

An inductive reasoning test is a common form of psychometric aptitude test used by employers, along with numerical and verbal reasoning. The most common form of inductive reasoning test involves spotting patterns in a series of graphics and finding the best match for the next in a sequence. Unlike deductive puzzles (such as Sudoku) where you can examine and discount possible outcomes one by one, inductive puzzles (such as cryptic crosswords) require you to create general conclusions from observable events and then test them. The reasoning is open and explorative.

Visual reasoning tests often include similar features: items rotating, items being mirrored, details of a shape being added or subtracted (e.g. shapes adding or losing a side). Also, there may be as many as five separate rules governing the behaviour of the items to create the pattern. If you can break down each puzzle into its components to identify individual rules, you can quickly narrow down possible solutions.

Here there is only one rule: the shape loses one straight line every time.

So the next in the series is

Now another rule has been added: the small shape alternates between being a triangle and a square.

So the next in the series is

Finally, a third rule has been added: there is a cross when both shapes have the same number of sides and a nought when they have different numbers of sides.

So the next in the series is

WHICH COMES NEXT IN THE SEQUENCE?

Look at the first five boxes, then choose the next in the series from boxes A–E.

1.

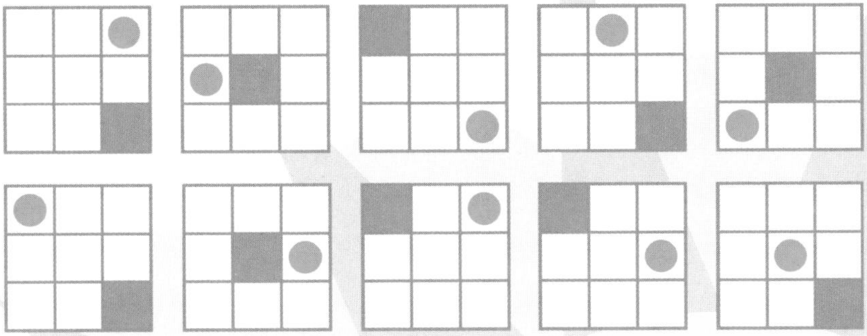

A   B   C   D   E

2.

A   B   C   D   E

3.

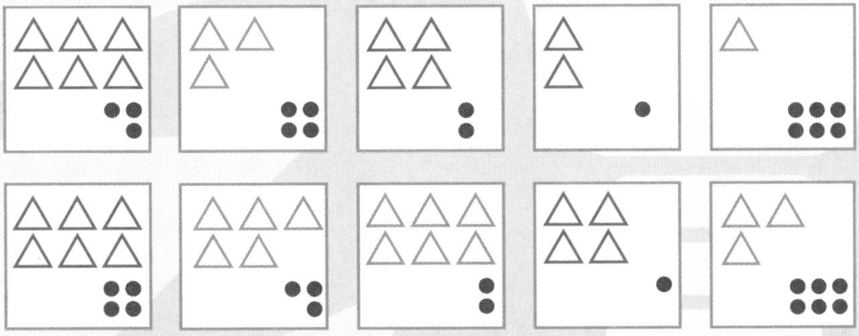

A   B   C   D   E

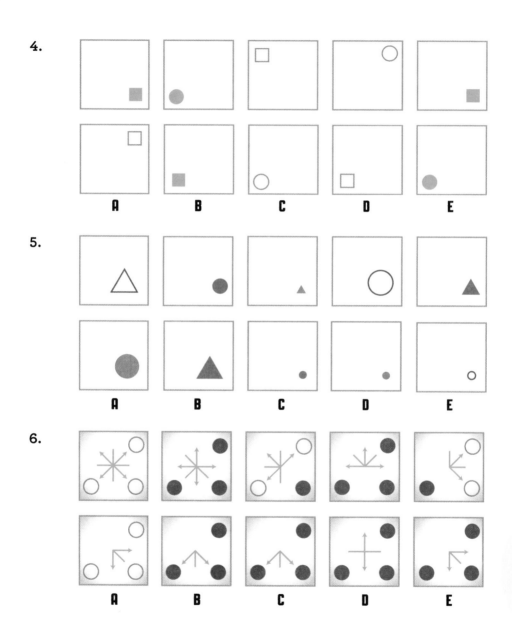

4.

A B C D E

5.

A B C D E

6.

A B C D E

7.

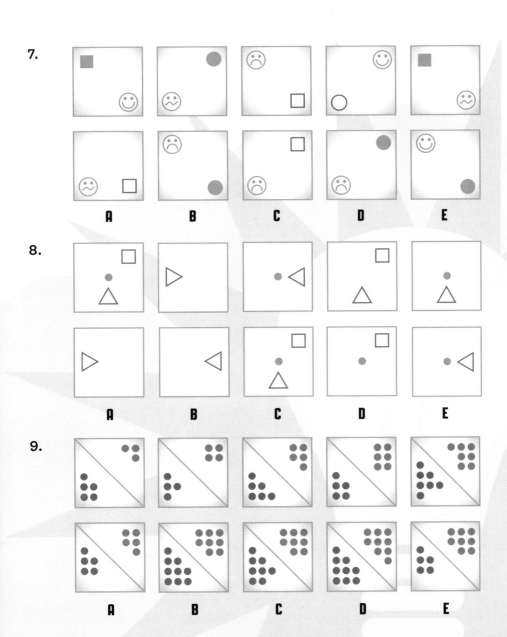

8.

9.

ABDUCTIVE REASONING

Abductive reasoning involves using observation of data to theorize the best explanation as to the cause of an observable set of data. Unlike deductive reasoning, conclusions from abductive reasoning may be false because there may be other causes.

For example, if the lawn is wet you may use abductive validation to theorize that it has recently rained, since it is a known rule that when it rains the grass gets wet. However, this may be a false conclusion. The lawn may be wet from dew or someone may have watered it with a hose. However, rain still remains a highly plausible solution. If you do not own a hose and it's winter, your rain hypothesis becomes even more plausible – it remains the simplest, most economical and elegant explanation.

Despite infinite possible explanations for the hundreds of events that take place each day of our lives, we constantly use abductive reasoning to orient us in our surroundings. It's a reasoning shorthand that encourages us to disregard the irrelevant causes of events, otherwise we would be unable to function. On a purely functional level it wouldn't benefit us to infer from a wet lawn that aliens landed in a spaceship with water pistols; it's imaginative, but from an abductive perspective it's a highly implausible explanation. More valid hypotheses are given priority to save time and effort so we can get on with our busy lives.

A syllogistic representation of abductive reasoning is:

The fact C is observed;

But if A were true, C would be a matter of course;

Hence, there is reason to suspect that A is true.

The most direct application of abduction is to find faults in systems. When a problem is observed, abduction can be used to derive a set of faults that are likely to have caused it. It is used in medical diagnosis and in legal reasoning, although watch out for errors caused by, for example, 'base rate fallacy' and 'prosecutor's fallacy'.

BASE RATE FALLACY

1. Police officers use roadside breathalysers that show a false drunkenness five per cent of the time, but they are 100 per cent reliable at detecting a genuinely drunk driver. One in two thousand drivers is driving over the legal limit. If a policeman stopped a driver at random and the breathalyser indicates that he or she is over the legal limit, what is the probability that this reading is genuine?

   a) lower than 1 per cent

   b) 95 per cent

   c) 96 per cent

2. A city has 1 million inhabitants of which 100 are terrorists. Facial recognition surveillance equipment in the city is designed to trigger an alarm every time it detects a terrorist. However, there are two bugs in the software:

   Bug 1: False negative: if the camera scans a terrorist it will only trigger the alarm 99 per cent of the time.

   Bug 2: False positive: if the camera scans a non-terrorist it will incorrectly trigger the alarm 1 per cent of the time.

   The alarm sounds. What is the approximate probability that the inhabitant is a terrorist?

   a) 99 per cent

   b) less than 1 per cent

   c) 98 per cent

PROSECUTOR'S FALLACY

A man is on trial for murder. The defendant shares the same rare blood type as the perpetrator (blood was found at the crime scene) and just 1 per cent of the population of 300 million. Setting all other evidence aside, what is the probability that the man is guilty based on the blood type match alone?

a) 10 per cent

b) 99 per cent

c) 0.00003333 per cent

BOOLEAN LOGIC

Boolean logic is a subarea of algebra that was originally developed in the nineteenth century by the English mathematician, philosopher and logician, George Boole.

The elementary algebra we learn at school uses variables to denote mainly numbers (e.g. $x^2 + 2y = z$) and the main operations are addition, subtraction, multiplication and division. In Boolean algebra the variables are the truth values TRUE (1) and FALSE (0) and the three fundamental operations are AND ($\wedge$), OR ($\vee$) and NOT ($\neg$).

AND ($\wedge$)

This operator takes two inputs and returns a 'true' (1) output only when BOTH of the inputs are true (1).

So if you have the inputs A and B and perform the operation AND on them (A $\wedge$ B) there are four possible combinations, but only one of them produces a 'true' (1) result.

A	B	A $\wedge$ B
False (0)	False (0)	False (0)
False (0)	True (1)	False (0)
True (1)	False (0)	False (0)
True (1)	True (1)	True (1)

OR ($\vee$)

This operator takes two inputs and returns a 'true' (1) output when ONE or BOTH of the inputs are true.

A	B	A $\vee$ B
False (0)	False (0)	False (0)
False (0)	True (1)	True (1)
True (1)	False (0)	True (1)
True (1)	True (1)	True (1)

NOT (¬)

This operator takes an input and returns the OPPOSITE so a 'true' (1) input returns a 'false' (0) output and a 'false' (0) input returns a 'true' (1) output.

A	A¬
False (0)	True (1)
True (1)	False (0)

These three operators are then combined to create more complex digital circuits.

So, for example, the statement 'If A and B are true or C is true, then Q is true' could be expressed with this truth table, showing all the possible combinations:

A	B	C	Q (A ∧ B ∨ C)
False (0)	False (0)	False (0)	False (0)
False (0)	False (0)	True (1)	True (1)
False (0)	True (1)	False (0)	False (0)
False (0)	True (1)	True (1)	True (1)
True (1)	False (0)	False (0)	False (0)
True (1)	False (0)	True (1)	True (1)
True (1)	True (1)	False (0)	True (1)
True (1)	True (1)	True (1)	True (1)

So what is the practical application? Boolean logic is the basis for modern digital computers. Here are two examples of Boolean logic at work:

FIZZY DRINK DISPENSER

A = Coin is inserted

B = Drink button is pressed

The programme inside the machine knows that when A and B occur (A ∧ B), it should dispense a drink (Q). The circuit uses a simple AND operation to decide whether or not to dispense a drink. Both events must be true for Q to take place.

THE FAMOUS TWO DOORS PUZZLE

You are faced with two doors and two guards. One guard always tells the truth and the other guard always lies. You don't know which guard is which. One door leads to Heaven, the other to Hell. You must choose a guard and may ask just one question to which the guard may only reply 'Yes' or 'No'.

Most people are familiar with this puzzle. It has appeared in various forms in popular culture including the *Doctor Who* story 'Pyramids of Mars' and the film *Labyrinth*. The question you should ask is 'If I asked the other guard if this door leads to Heaven, what would he tell me?'

Using the AND operation, it is clear that you will only get a true result when all the constituent variables are true and a false result otherwise. In other words, the only way you can guarantee a truthful answer is if both guards told the truth. Since you know this isn't the case and also, that both guards can't be liars, the only remaining options return a false result. So, if the guard says 'yes', you should choose the other door; if the guard says 'no', you should choose that door.

Guard A	Guard B	A ^ B
False (0)	False (0)	False (0)
False (0)	**True (1)**	**False (0)**
True (1)	**False (0)**	**False (0)**
True (1)	True (1)	True (1)

THESE PUZZLES CAN ALSO BE SOLVED USING BOOLEAN LOGIC

1. Inspector Hercule Poirot interrogates two suspects of the theft of the Hope Diamond.

    Bonnie declares: Both Clyde and I are guilty.

    Clyde protests: Bonnie stole it.

    If one of them is lying and the other one is telling the truth, who stole the diamond?

2. John says: My wife and I are both liars.

    Who is what?

3. There are three boxes. One is labelled 'NUTS', another is labelled 'BOLTS' and the third is labelled 'NUTS AND BOLTS'. You know that each box is labelled incorrectly. You may pick just one item from one single box. How can you label the boxes correctly?

GEOMETRIC REASONING

Geometry is a branch of mathematics that focuses upon shape, size, relative position of figures and the properties of space. It first developed in several ancient cultures to deal with everyday issues such as lengths, areas and volumes and it began to emerge in the West as a formal mathematical discipline in the sixth century BC with Thales, one of the Seven Sages of ancient Greece. The word 'geometry' derives from the Greek *geo* (earth) and *metron* (measure).

The acknowledged Father of Geometry was the Greek mathematician Euclid, who worked in Alexandria, Egypt, in the third century BC. His 13-volume *Elements* is one of the most important books in the history of mathematics. Euclid was the first mathematician to write down a small group of axioms and then use them to deduce many other propositions. An axiom is a statement which is regarded as being self-evidently true and it is the product of inductive reasoning (*see* page 32). Euclid based his entire system of geometry on just five axioms and five 'common notions'.

AXIOMS

1. A straight line can be drawn between any two points.

2. A finite line can be extended infinitely in both directions.

3. A circle can be drawn with any centre and any radius.

4. All right angles are equal to each other.

5. Given a line and a point not on the line, only one line can be drawn through the point parallel to the line.

COMMON NOTIONS

1. Things which are equal to the same thing are also equal to one another.

2. If equals are added to equals, the wholes are equal.

3. If equals are subtracted from equals, the remainders are equal.

4. Things which coincide with one another are equal to one another.

5. The whole is greater than the part.

The fifth axiom, known as the 'parallel postulate', became famous because mathematicians spent the next two thousand years trying to prove it. Finally, in the early nineteenth century, a young Hungarian prodigy named János Bolyai moved beyond the parallel postulate and the results were quite literally explosive.

Bolyai had spent more than ten years obsessed with Euclid's parallel postulate. In 1832, at the age of 30, he published a treatise describing his system of revolutionary non-Euclidian geometry based on a different description of parallel lines. 'I created a new, different world out of nothing' he wrote to his father, which was an understatement.

Russian mathematician Nikolai Lobachevsky had also published a similar piece of work three years earlier. The Bolyai–Lobachevsky departure from Euclid, along with the work of the contemporary 55-year-old German genius Carl Friedrich Gauss (who had also been obsessed with the problem for 35 years), was a colossal mathematical breakthrough.

Thanks to Bolyai–Lobachevsky and Gauss, the mathematical tools existed to enable Einstein to develop the idea of curved space-time and his Theory of General Relativity, which in turn led to the creation of the atomic bomb.

GEOMETRICAL MAGIC

Geometry is an awesome tool that allows mathematicians to become the creators and destroyers of worlds. Or for those whose ambitions are more modest, it allows us to create and perform some baffling magic tricks, including the famous 64 = 65 Geometry Paradox:

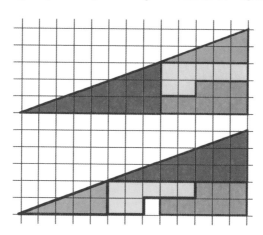

Where does the hole in the second triangle come from (the partitions are the same)?

Geometry can explain the apparent paradox. In fact, the edges of the four shapes do not lie along a straight line. The diagonal line is not a line at all; it is a shape – a lozenge (diamond-shaped figure) – whose area exactly matches the so-called 'missing' square.

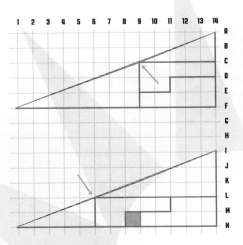

SEVEN GEOMETRY PUZZLES

Try tackling these geometric brain teasers. Don't worry – you don't need to have any prior knowledge of geometry.

1. A castle is surrounded by a moat that is 4 metres wide with a 90-degree turn. You have only two planks, each of which is 3.9 metres long. How can you cross the moat immediately using just the planks laid flat?

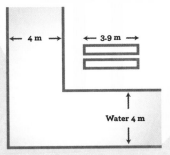

2. Place 10 balls in 5 lines in such a way that each line has exactly 4 balls on it.

3. Why is it better to have round manhole covers than square ones?

4. A hunter walks one kilometre south from his camp, then one kilometre west and shoots a bear. Then he walks one kilometre north and is back at his camp. What colour was the bear?

5. Imagine you had a piece of string that wrapped once around a basketball. If you were to add an extra metre of length to the string, there would be a gap of 15.92 cm between the ball and the string.

    Now imagine you had a piece of string that was long enough to wrap around the equator of the earth (40,075 km). If you were to add another 1 metre of length to this string, how high off the ground would the string be now?

    a) 15.92 cm

    b) 0.00000000000000001 cm

    c) 0.0000001 cm

    Hint: the only equation you need to solve this problem is $r = c/2\Pi$ (where r is the radius, and c is the circumference and Π is 3.14).

6. How can you create 8 equilateral triangles with 6 lolly sticks (without breaking any)?

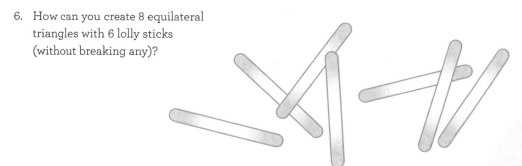

7. Four people go out for lunch and share a large pizza. They divide it into equal parts with five straight cuts and each gets three pieces. How?

SPATIAL THINKING

Spatial thinking is the ability to visualize with the mind's eye, to solve spatial problems, imagine and manipulate objects in space. It is crucial to problem solving and deeply embedded in the activities of daily life from filling the dishwasher to fitting a child safety seat into a car.

Some of the greatest thinkers in history possessed staggering powers of spatial visualization. Nikola Tesla, one of the greatest electrical inventors who ever lived, is reputed to have been able to visualize every part of a working engine in his mind and mentally test each component. Watson and Crick discovered the molecular structure of DNA by imagining and building a three-dimensional model to reveal that the long chain molecules form a double helix – marking one of the greatest achievements of twentieth-century science.

Research has shown that children and adults alike can improve their spatial thinking with practice. Even playing the block-manipulating computer game Tetris creates dramatic improvements in spatial thinking that are long-lasting and transferable to other situations.

1. TWO-DIMENSIONAL SPATIAL VISUALIZATION

Choose the drawing that matches the shape after it has been rotated 180 degrees.

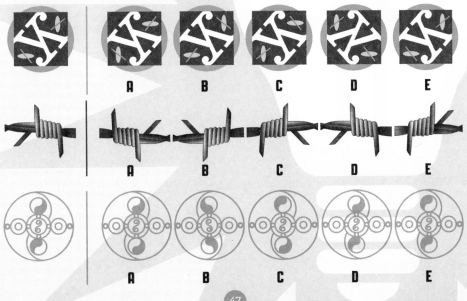

2. THREE-DIMENSIONAL SPATIAL VISUALIZATION

Which of the five objects can be assembled from the flat cardboard?

(Fold so the dotted lines are on the outside of the 3-D shape).

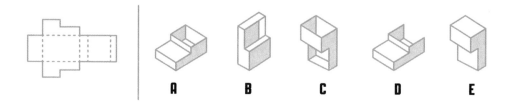

Only two of the shapes are identical to the original. Which are they?

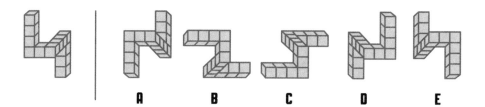

Which shape matches the original?

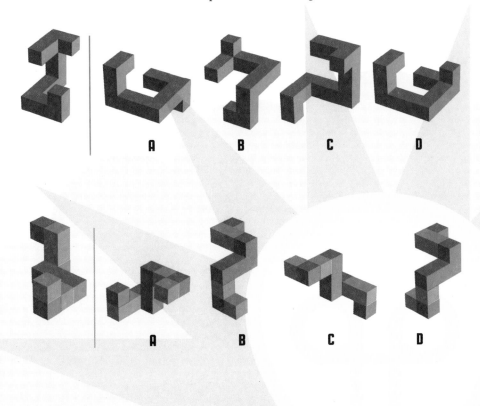

A   B   C   D

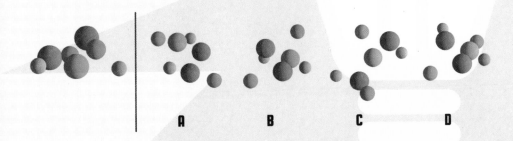

A   B   C   D

49

The three shapes below are standing on a glass table – what is the view looking up from below the table?

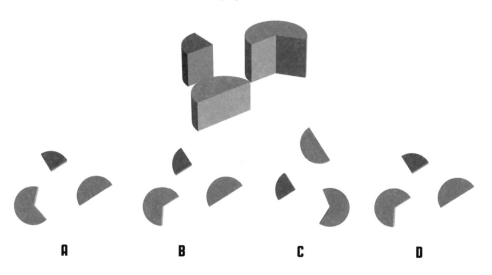

A   B   C   D

Which is the odd one out?

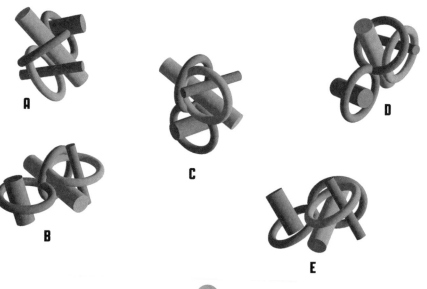

A

B

C

D

E

LATERAL THINKING

According to its inventor, the Maltese doctor and author Edward de Bono, the term 'lateral thinking' was created in 1967; it first appeared in his worldwide best-seller, *The Use of Lateral Thinking*.

The key principle behind lateral thinking can be summed up by his maxim: 'You cannot dig a hole in a different place by digging the same hole deeper' which means that you cannot solve a problem by repeating the same strategy (because the creative breakthrough is often the result of effort focused in a different direction). This requires you to change concepts and preconceptions: 'We assume certain perceptions, certain concepts and certain boundaries. Lateral thinking is concerned not with playing with the existing pieces but with seeking to change those very pieces.'

In school we are taught to face problems head-on using what de Bono calls 'vertical thinking' but the brain is 'a self-organizing information system' which 'forms asymmetric patterns' and 'in such systems there is a mathematical need for moving across patterns'. Lateral thinking aims to address this need.

LATERAL THINKING TECHNIQUES

Alternatives: Look for alternative solutions and concepts even when doing so isn't urgent. Looking beyond the obvious systemic solutions generates a network of creative branches to explore.

Focus: Make a deliberate effort to focus on areas that no one else has thought about.

Challenge current thinking: The 'If it ain't broke, don't fix it' mentality means that we don't question the status quo; we assume that the existing solutions are adequate because they appear to be working satisfactorily. However, if you break the inertia by working from the assumption that the current solution is not optimal, you can find a better solution that no one has bothered to consider before.

Random entry: Introduce random input to encourage new associations. For example, when brainstorming a problem or idea, open a book at a random page, pick a word and introduce that word into the thinking process; often the juxtaposition of the new word can unlock your creativity.

Provocation: Generate deliberately unreasonable, provocative or hyperbolic statements and use them to build new ideas.

Here is a classic example of a lateral thinking brain teaser with which you may already be familiar:

A father and his son have a car accident and the son is rushed to hospital for emergency surgery. The surgeon looks at him and says, 'I can't operate on him, he's my son.' Explain.

The surgeon is, of course, his mother. It is a classic illustration of how we can solve problems by challenging our assumptions and prejudices. Many lateral thinking problems are designed to exploit one or more assumptions, or they establish an initial detail that is overlooked when reading the whole problem. Here's a slightly different problem:

A trainee airline pilot had just completed a long-haul flight to Sydney when he met the captain wearing a dress in the hotel bar. What should he do?

Join her for a drink, maybe? Did you make the same gender stereotype mistake again? Different problem, same assumption!

Romeo and Juliet lie dead on the floor. There is water and glass strewn around their unclothed bodies. Why did they die?

Here we make the assumption that Romeo and Juliet are humans, which is reinforced by the word 'unclothed'. They are goldfish.

It's also important to read the question carefully. Many lateral thinking problems rely on the reader missing obvious details:

1. To the nearest cubic centimetre, how much soil is there in a 3 m x 2 m x 2 m hole?

2. A farmer has 15 cows; all but 8 die. How many does he have left?

3. John's mother has three children. One is named April, one is named May. What is the third one named?

If your answers are 12 m^2, 7 and June, reread the questions – slowly.

Our assumptions are usually the product of abductive reasoning (*see* page 38) which is useful in day-to-day situations, but a hindrance when trying to think laterally.

Can you solve these conundrums with some lateral thinking? Beware – some of the answers are rather outlandish!

1. Name an ancient invention still in use in most parts of the world today that allows people to see through walls.

2. Deep in the forest a man's body was found. He was wearing only swimming trunks, snorkel and facemask. The nearest lake was 10 kilometres away and the sea was 100 kilometres away. How did he die?

3. A man dies of thirst in his own home. How?

4. How could a toddler fall out of a thirty-storey building onto the ground and survive?

5. A man wants to build a house, so he asks for quotes from one hundred builders, each of which claims to be the best builder in the area. Getting the best builder possible is more important to him than price, so how does he choose between them?

6. A seven-foot-tall man is holding a glass beaker above his head. He drops it on the carpet without spilling a single drop of water. How?

7. A traffic cop sees a lorry driver going the wrong way down a one-way street, but doesn't arrest him. Why?

8. A man is found dead in a field. He is holding a broken match. What happened?

9. There are six eggs in the basket. Six people each take one of the eggs but one egg is left in the basket. How can this be?

10. A man drank some of the punch at a party, then he left early. Everyone else who drank the punch died of poisoning, but the man was unharmed. Why?

11. When Archduke Ferdinand was shot, his attendants could not undo his coat to stop the bleeding. Why not? (True story.)

12. A man lies dead in a room. There is a net basket on the floor containing gold and jewels, a chandelier attached to the ceiling and a large open window. How did he die?

13. Tommy's mother told him never to open the cellar door. One day while she was out, the cellar door opened and Tommy saw a man kneeling and smiling at him. What was the man wearing?

14. A woman called the waiter in a restaurant. She told him there was a fly in her tea. The waiter took it away and brought her a fresh cup. After a few moments the woman knew it was the same cup of tea. How?

15. What happened in the year 1961 that won't occur again for almost another 4,000 years?

16. A man was walking downstairs in a building when he suddenly realized that his wife had just died. How?

17. How long is a piece of string?

18. Acting on an anonymous tip-off, police raid a house to arrest a suspected terrorist. All they know is that his name is Joaquín and that he is inside the building. Inside the house they find a carpenter, a lorry driver, a mechanic, a wrestler, an astronaut and a man with a beard all playing poker. They immediately arrest the bearded man. How did they know he was the terrorist?

19. Two drivers stop at a traffic light which is showing red. A nearby police officer immediately arrests one of the drivers. Why?

20. Why did an old lady always answer the door wearing her hat and coat?

21. A blind beggar had a brother who died. What relation was the blind beggar to the brother who died? (Brother is not the answer.)

22. If a plane crashes on the Italian/Swiss border, where do you bury the survivors?

23. As I was going to St Ives, I met a man with seven wives; Each wife had seven sacks; Each sack had seven cats; Each cat had seven kits: Kits, cats, sacks and wives; How many were going to St Ives?

24. A man is lying dead in a field. Next to him there is an unopened package. There is no other animal in the field. How did he die?

25. The music stopped. She died. Explain.

26. A man walks into a bar and asks for a glass of water. The barman pulls out a gun and points it at the man. The man thanks him and walks out. Why?

27. The most boring man in the world was on his way home in a taxi. The taxi driver pretended to be deaf and dumb so he wouldn't have to engage him in conversation. They reached the destination, the most boring man in the world paid the fare and opened his front door. Then he realized that the taxi driver had been pretending. How?

28. Alison lives in a remote part of the Australian outback. She wants a tattoo so she visits the only two tattoo artists for 500 kilometres. Both of them are covered in impressive tattoos, but the clincher is a magnificent eagle, with wings outstretched between the shoulder blades of the second tattoo artist. Despite this demonstration of breathtaking artistry, she decides to hire the first one instead. Why?

PARALLEL THINKING

Parallel thinking is another technique that was invented by the Maltese doctor and author Edward de Bono. The system is the direct opposite of dialectic or adversarial methods which take the form of argument and counter-argument, the most famous of which is Socratic debate.

In Socratic debate, a discussion takes place between two or more individuals, based on asking and answering questions that challenge and explore beliefs in an attempt to highlight inconsistencies within a particular viewpoint. This leads to better hypotheses that are based on reason, rather than what the classical Greek philosopher Socrates considered to be the rhetoric and clever oratorical and philosophical tricks employed by the sophists, who preceded him.

Parallel thinking is more collaborative and non-confrontational. Several thinkers put forward hypotheses and ideas in parallel, helping to guide the discussion in one direction at a time so that each issue can be explored more fully, rather than try to score points over opponents or charm them with clever oratory.

The most famous parallel thinking (or multiperspective analysis) system is de Bono's 'Six Thinking Hats' method. When faced with a problem, one by one put on each of the differently coloured thinking hats and approach the problem from a different viewpoint.

White Hat: Facts and figures
This is the number crunching, data collecting, researching hat that gathers all the available information related to the issue. It looks at past trends and analyses previous results/performance. It asks what information you have and what more information you need.

Red Hat: Emotions and feelings
The wearer of this hat approaches the problem using intuition, emotion and gut instinct. It also looks outwards to other people and empathizes with their feelings and opinions.

Black Hat: Cautious and careful
Wearing the black hat makes you anticipate obstacles, negative consequences and risks and explore contingency plans. It focuses solely on weak points, failures and underperformance. De Bono has said that within the context of the other five hats, the black hat can be the most productive, and help to counter too much yellow hat thinking.

Green Hat: Creative thinking

The green hat looks for creative solutions, alternatives, new ideas and possibilities. It is non-judgemental and does not self-censor.

Yellow Hat: Speculative-Positive

Wearing the yellow hat makes you see only the positives and the benefits; it mitigates risks and views obstacles as challenges to be overcome. However, it isn't just blind optimism, since it should still be supported by analytical and strategic thinking.

Blue Hat: Control of thinking

The blue hat is process control. It sets out the agenda, maintains group focus, oversees the other hats and acts as a chairperson, helping to consolidate information, note conclusions and formulate action points.

HERE ARE TEN QUESTIONS TO WHICH YOU SHOULD APPLY PARALLEL THINKING TO FIND A SOLUTION:

1. How can I get myself a 25 per cent pay rise?

2. How can I improve by two levels at school?

3. How can I find someone to spend the rest of my life with?

4. Should I stay in this marriage and try to work things out?

5. What's the best way to improve my health and well-being?

6. Should we have another baby?

7. How can I free up some leisure time?

8. What are five effective ways to do my bit for the environment?

9. Where should I go on holiday next year?

10. Should I buy a dog?

SIMPLE SOLUTIONS
ARE BEST

Human delight in simplicity is ubiquitous and is expressed in every discipline from philosophy, epistemology (the study of the theory of knowledge) and theology to science and art. According to St Thomas Aquinas, 'God is infinitely simple'. The Italian Renaissance polymath Leonardo da Vinci considered simplicity to be 'the ultimate sophistication'. Scientists often talk about scientific and mathematical theories being beautiful and simple and they aim to make them as simple as possible without sacrificing accuracy or crucial meaning.

Albert Einstein famously said, 'If you can't explain it to a six-year-old, you don't understand it yourself.' This is worth bearing in mind whenever you are grappling with complex ideas.

The heuristic that simple solutions are the best is often referred to as 'Occam's Razor', named after William of Ockham, the medieval English Franciscan friar who invented it. It is the principle that when you have competing hypotheses, you should choose the one with the fewest assumptions and variable parameters. The more assumptions that you make and the more adjustable parameters you introduce, the greater the possibility for error and inaccuracy in the end result.

As we have seen in earlier chapters (*see* pages 32 and 38), our preference for simplicity is a fundamental component of inductive and abductive reasoning but just because something is simple doesn't mean that it is always right and, conversely, just because something is complicated doesn't mean we should dismiss it out of hand. One of the main arguments that Creationists make against the theory of evolution is that it couldn't create creatures of such variety and detail. Of course, the irony is that the theory's simplicity is its greatest strength and accounts for why nature can be so complicated and how life on earth has developed from single-celled organisms to creatures of increasing complexity.

Isaac Newton's Theory of Gravity has been superseded by Einstein's Theory of General Relativity and ever more complex theories such as Superstring Theory, but it is still used because it is simpler and still gives sufficiently accurate results for many gravitational calculations. So even when a simple solution is replaced by a more complex one, we have a preference for simplicity over accuracy to solve everyday problems.

So, despite its limitations, Occam's Razor or the acronym KISS (keep it simple, stupid) still remain useful principles to follow when you are trying to solve problems and puzzles. But if a more complex system does a better job, use that one instead. Don't get so hung up on simplicity that you avoid complexity. Maybe the best way to approach Occam's Razor is to follow the advice of twentieth-century English mathematician and philosopher, Alfred North Whitehead, the founder of the philosophical school known as process philosophy, who advised: 'Seek simplicity and distrust it.'

THE SEVEN BRIDGES OF KÖNIGSBERG

The old town of Königsberg has seven bridges. Can you take a walk through the town, fully crossing each bridge once and only once? (You may only cross a river by bridge. No jumping or swimming allowed!)

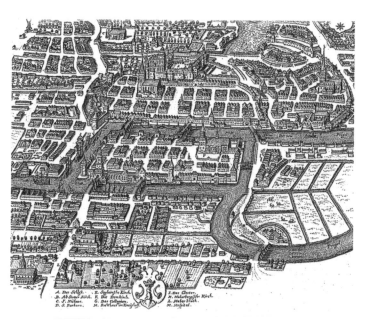

FIVE ROOM PUZZLE

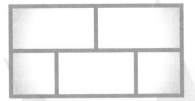

A large rectangular house is divided into five rooms. Can a ghost walk through each wall in a continuous line only once?

FOUR FORWARD-THINKING CAMELS

Four forward-thinking camels were travelling along a very narrow mountainside ledge when they encountered another four forward-thinking camels approaching from the opposite direction. Everyone knows that forward-thinking camels have no reverse gear, but they will climb over another camel, so long as there is a camel-sized space on the other side.

Both camel quartets stop, facing each other, with exactly one camel's width between them. How can all the camels continue on their journey without any camel reversing (or jumping off the ledge)?

These puzzles are a good illustration that simple solutions are the best. The smarter you are and the higher your level of formal education, the more difficulty you will have calculating the answer. So keep your reasoning simple.

1. How can you throw a ball as hard as you can and ensure that it comes back to you even if it doesn't hit anything, there is no string or elastic attached to it and no one else throws or catches it?

2. What is the pattern here? bun, stew, ghee, pour, chive, mix, leaven, weight, dine, hen.

3. Copernican Revolution

The first roll of the dice scores two.

The second roll of the dice scores six.

The third roll of the dice scores zero.

The fourth roll of the dice scores ten.

The fifth roll of the dice scores four.

What does this score?

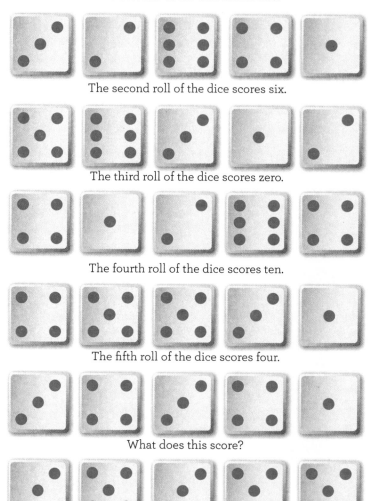

VERBAL REASONING

Verbal reasoning is thinking with words, the ability to understand written information and to make reasoned conclusions using concepts framed in language. The ability to think constructively is even more important than language fluency (*see* page 65) and vocabulary knowledge (*see* page 70) and it is more than simply being good at literacy.

Verbal reasoning tests are widely used by employers and you can significantly improve your score with practice; there are scores of sample tests available online (google 'verbal reasoning tests'). The tests are time restricted, so familiarity with the format will allow you to focus solely on your performance and give you a distinct advantage over more confident candidates with innate ability but less preparation.

When completing a verbal reasoning test, follow these five tips:

1. KEEP CALM

Verbal reasoning tests are usually timed, which adds pressure, so apart from practice, staying calm is the single most important way to maintain focus and boost your performance. No one can concentrate when they are agitated, so control your emotions.

2. READ THE STATEMENT TWO OR THREE TIMES

Don't rush. If you rush the reading stage and start answering the questions too early, you will waste more time rereading because you haven't assimilated the finer details. It's more time efficient to read the passage three times at the beginning, rather than have to keep returning to the text later. However, you may benefit from quickly skimming the passage once to pick out key words and to provide context, before making your 2–3 detailed readings.

3. MAKE SENSE OF CONVOLUTED TEXT BY STARTING AT THE END OF THE SENTENCE

This trick helps you understand complicated sentences containing several sub-clauses.

4. DON'T WASTE ALL YOUR TIME ON ONE QUESTION

If you are really stuck, move on to the next question; it's better to drop one point than ten. You don't lose marks for skipping questions.

5. MAKE NO ASSUMPTIONS

Only reason using information contained within the text. This is NOT a test of your general knowledge.

1. Three words are related and two do NOT go with the other three – which two?

   angle, fish, pushover, tackle, rugby   Answer: _____   _____

   dough, maiden, crimp, whisk, duck   Answer: _____   _____

   chinook, confluence, drizzle, gale, precipitate   Answer: _____   _____

2. Find a common single word that goes with each trio to form a new word or phrase:

blue	motion	drop
cake	worm	off
cottage	down	stand

   _____   _____   _____

3. PREVARICATE is to EVADE as TAXONOMY is to:

   a) vary

   b) innovation

   c) modulation

   d) development

   e) classification

4. Which two words are closest in meaning?

   SOPORIFIC, MAUDLIN, SOOTHING, EXHAUSTED, APOLOGETIC

5. Which two words are the most nearly opposite in meaning?

   TRIBULATION, ADMONISH, CONTENTMENT, REPROVE, EXHORT

6. Add one letter to each word to find two areas that are susceptible to flooding.

   MASH   SWAP

7. What is the longest word that can be produced from these ten letters?

   ICAEORTSAB

8. Solve the clues to find five six-letter words. The same three-letter word is represented by 123 in each case.

1 2 3 * * *	box or container
* 1 2 3 * *	Egyptian amulet
* * 1 2 3 *	ecclesiastic representatives
* * * 1 2 3	surgical instrument

9. Solve the puzzle using one letter:

hrif

ypis

orren

antamoun

10. Solve the puzzle using the same two letters for all the words in each list:

uli	_ande_
eacu	_appe_
oysho	_ephy_
reeto	_ippe_
rollo	_ithe_

11. Solve the puzzle using the same three letters for all the words in each list:

_i_h_p	_d_g_os
_i_s_l	_t_v_sm
_i_l_y	_c_c_as
	_v_r_ce

12. You have five minutes to read the passage and answer the ten questions below.

Returning to civilian life he took up his quest again, varying a general medical and surgical practice by continued observation and experiment in gland-transplantations upon animals, leaning ever more strongly towards the exclusive use of goats. About this time he heard of the work of Professor Steinach of Vienna in grafting the glands of rats, and producing changes in the character and appearance of the animals by inverting the process of nature and transplanting male glands into females, and vice versa, sometimes with success. He had followed with the greatest interest also the experiments of Dr Frank Lydston of Chicago, who performed his first human-gland transplantation upon himself, an example of courage that falls not far short of heroism. But Dr Brinkley was never favourably impressed with the idea of using the glands of a human being for the renovation of the life-force of another human being. He was looking to the young of the animal kingdom to furnish him with the material he proposed to use to improve the functioning of human organs, and more certainly as time passed he drew to the conclusion that in the goat, and in the goat alone, was to be found that gland-tissue which, because of its rapid maturity, potency, and freedom from those diseases to which humanity is liable, was most sure under right conditions of implantation to feed, nourish, grow into and become a part of, human gland-tissue.

[*The Goat-Gland Transplantation* by Sydney B. Flower, 1921]

Answer using a, b or c:

    a) True (the statement follows logically from the information contained in the passage)

    b) False (the statement is logically false from the information contained in the passage)

    c) Cannot say (cannot determine whether the statement is true or false without further information)

1. Dr Brinkley had experimented with gland transplantation upon animals other than goats in the past.
2. Dr Frank Lydston performed the first human-gland transplantation.
3. Dr Brinkley considered Professor Steinach a hero.
4. Dr Brinkley reached the conclusion that the goat was the only animal from which it was suitable to harvest glands capable of becoming a part of human gland-tissue.
5. Dr Brinkley heard about the work of Professor Steinach of Vienna before his return to civilian life.
6. Dr Brinkley strongly disapproved of the work of Dr Frank Lydston.
7. Professor Steinach had some success in transplanting glands between male and female goats.
8. Steinach exclusively transplanted male glands into females.
9. Dr Brinkley liked Dr Frank Lydston.
10. Dr Frank Lydston and Dr Brinkley had never met in person.

VERBAL FLUENCY

Verbal fluency relies on semantic (meaning) memory and phonemic (word sounds) memory. It is measured by a verbal fluency test which generally involves listing as many different items in a group as possible within a time limit – often one minute.

Neuropsychological research shows that this task activates both frontal and temporal lobe areas of the brain. The frontal lobe is important for the phonemic component and the temporal lobe processes the semantic modifications. Tests on thousands of people – children and adults – have revealed that healthy individuals share several performance characteristics:

1. The rate at which new words are produced declines hyperbolically during the test.

2. Most of us say the more obvious words early on in the test (and repeat them more often) before moving on to less common words.

3. We produce clusters of words, linked by meaning and sound. If the category was 'animal', saying 'cow' usually triggers a cascade of farm animals – 'sheep, pig, goat' – and saying 'cat' leads to a cluster of domestic pets – 'dog, rabbit, bird, hamster, mouse, gerbil, goldfish'.

The diagram is a cluster analysis of animal semantic fluency data from 55 British schoolchildren aged 7–8. Notice that the animals cluster according to the environmental context in which they are observed – **farm, home, ocean, zoo**. This cluster pattern forms in childhood and stays with us for the rest of our lives. Verbal fluency tests on adults and even zoology PhD students have produced identical schematic results.

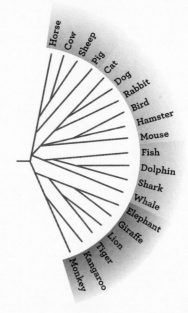

The patterns of recall are so predictable that deviation from these norms is usually a sign of cognitive impairment, caused by brain injury (especially lesions on the frontal lobe) or neurological conditions and disorders. So verbal fluency tests are a useful clinical diagnostic tool and are quite accurate in screening for dementia.

The COWAT (Controlled Oral Word Association Task) is a cognitive test of verbal processing ability used to assess brain impairment. The most common letters chosen are F, A and S. A score of under 17 indicates concern, although some physicians use 14 as a cut-off.

1. PERFORM YOUR OWN CLUSTER ANALYSIS

Take a group of friends, work colleagues or members of your family and give them one minute to silently write down a vertical list of as many animals as they can. Now compare the results and you will see this clustering at work.

2. ELEPHANTS IN DENMARK

This trick relies on this memory clustering phenomenon and some mathematical direction to showcase your mind-reading ability.

Read this to your audience, pausing between instructions to give them time to make the necessary calculations:

1. Pick a number between 2 and 9. It can be 2 or it can be 9, or any number in between.

2. Multiply your number by 9.

3. Now you have a two-digit number. Add the digits together.

4. Subtract 5.

5. Now find the letter that corresponds with your result. A = 1, B = 2, C = 3, etc.

6. Think of a country that begins with your letter. For example, 'C' might make you think of Canada or 'F' could be France.

7. Take the second letter in the name of that country and think of an animal.

8. Now close your eyes and visualize your animal while I read your mind.

9. Say, 'I DIDN'T KNOW THAT THERE WERE ELEPHANTS IN DENMARK.'

THE HUMAN
SPELLCHECKER

If you rely on the spellchecker on your word processing software to spot all your typos and clumsy grammar and to generally compensate for your sloppiness or fat finger syndrome, you'll have no doubt learned the hard way that there is no substitute for good old-fashioned human spellchecking. It doesn't matter how sophisticated automatic spellchecking becomes – errors of omission, transposition or substitution as well as specialist words are overlooked.

Read any modern novel and the visual barrage of typos suggests that even major publishing houses place too much trust in their digital spellchecker or hire incompetent proofreaders.

Whether you are applying for a job, making a presentation or writing for a website, the importance of spelling cannot be overestimated. Spelling mistakes destroy credibility and cost you money, not least when your expensive 'Nitendo console' or 'Tomy Hilfiger' jacket sells for 99 pence on eBay because you didn't bother to check the spelling. Every day hundreds of eBay auctions are created with misspelt titles, and lots of free websites exploit this by finding spelling mistakes so savvy shoppers can grab a bargain and profit from other people's carelessness.

Use these proofreading tips whenever you have finished a piece of work (don't proofread if you plan to rewrite or edit further):

1. Take a break. Set aside for at least an hour, preferably 24 hours.

2. Print a paper copy. People read differently on screen and are more inclined to skim and miss errors.

3. Read out slowly, aloud and telegraphically – one word at a time and almost robotically, rather than using the natural flowing cadence of speech. This helps you to see what is actually there, rather than what the context and flow might fool you into thinking is there.

4. Read with the expectation that you will find mistakes. You will spot mistakes more easily if you assume they are there. Be happy when you spot a mistake (rather than frustrated that you made it) to motivate you to continue proofreading ever more carefully.

5. Focus on one element of your writing at a time. For example, you might read once for sense, then a second and third time for spelling and punctuation without thinking about the content or story.

6. Watch for contractions and apostrophes. If you don't know the rules, then learn them once and for all RIGHT NOW and you'll never be in doubt again:

   - Apostrophes are NEVER used to form plurals, even when using abbreviations (e.g. the plural of DVD is DVDs).
   - It is, there is, is not, he is, she is, I am – anything where two words are contracted, uses an apostrophe – it's, there's, isn't, he's, she's, I'm.
   - Apostrophes are used in the possessive except with its, your, yours, hers, our, ours, theirs. The apostrophe comes before the s with singular and after the s with plural (the dog's ball = one dog, the dogs' ball = more than one dog).

7. Watch for repetitions (the the, a, a), transposed words or letters and homonyms (words that sound the same but are spelled differently); these won't be detected by a spellchecker: words like from/form, their/there, house/horse.

8. If in doubt, assume you've made a mistake. Make a note and CHECK in a dictionary or grammar book.

9. Create a list of your common mistakes and read it before you begin so your brain is primed to look out for them.

Read the passage (excerpted from Chapter Two of *Wuthering Heights* by Emily Brontë) and see if you can spot fifteen errors.

On opening the little door, two hairy monsters flew at my throat, bearing me down, and extinguishing the light; while a mingled guffaw form Heathcliffe and Hareton put the copestone on my rage and humilation. Fortunately, the beast seemed more bent on stretching there paws, and yawning, and flourishing their tails, then devouring me alive; but they would suffer no resurection, and I was forced to lie till their malignant masters pleased to deliver me: then, hatless and trembling with wrath, I ordered the miscreants to let me out – on their peril to keep me me one minute longer – with several incoherent threats of retaliation that, in their indefinite depth of virulency, smacked of King Lear.

The vehemence of my agitation brought on a copious bleeding at the nose, and still Heathcliff laughed, and still I scalded. I don't know what would have concluded the scene, had their not been one person at hand rather more rational then myself, and more benevolent than my entertainer. This was Zillah, the stout housewife; who at length issued fourth to inquire into the the nature of the uproar. She though that some of them had been lying violent hands on me; and, not daring to attack her master, she turned her vocal artillery against the younger scoundrel.

This internet meme demonstrates how easily we understand meaning in text, despite typos. It helps to explain why so many typos go unnoticed by the casual reader.

Cdnuolt blveiee taht I cluod aulaclty uesdnatnrd waht I was rdanieg. The phaonmneal pweor of the hmuan mnid. Aoccdrnig to rscheearch at Cmabrigde Uinervtisy, it deosn't mttaer in waht oredr the ltteers in a wrod are, the olny iprmoatnt tihng is taht the frist and lsat ltteer be in the rghit pclae. The rset can be a taotl mses and you can sitll raed it wouthit a porbelm. Tihs is bcuseae the huamn mnid deos not raed ervey lteter by istlef, but the wrod as a wlohe. Amzanig huh? Yaeh and I awlyas tghuhot slpeling was ipmorantt!

They Say:
You don't know what you've got till it's gone.

Truth:
You knew exactly what what you had; you just thought you'd never lose it.

Many readers are not aware that the the brain will automatically ignore a second instance of a short word like 'what' when it it starts a new line.

Now go back and read that last last sentence slowly and telegraphically one more time.

Now reread the sentence before this one. Did you spot that 'what' was repeated (what you had) then 'the' (the brain) was repeated then 'it' (it starts a new line) and finally 'last' (last sentence)?

VOCABULARY

IN MID-JUNE 2009 US COMPANY GLOBAL LANGUAGE MONITOR (GLM) ANNOUNCED ITS BELIEF THAT THE ONE MILLIONTH WORD HAD BEEN ADDED TO THE ENGLISH LANGUAGE (ALTHOUGH OTHER ESTIMATES PUT THIS FIGURE CLOSER TO TWO MILLION AND THAT'S NOT INCLUDING THE 600,000 KNOWN SPECIES OF FUNGUS). THEY ESTIMATE A NEW WORD IS CREATED EVERY 98 MINUTES.

We have so many words from which to choose and yet most adults only use a few thousand in their active daily speech (although nearly everyone knows at least 35,000 words and many people know more than 100,000). But there is a well-established correlation between a wide vocabulary and success.

Champion Scrabble players have some of the highest recognition vocabularies of anyone in the world. Former UK Scrabble champion Allan Simmons claims he can recognize around 100,000 of the 160,000 words of nine letters or under included on the Scrabble list.

The best way to grow a large working vocabulary is to grow up in a language-rich environment surrounded by books and with parents who read, read to their children and encourage them to read. It's never too late to learn. Building your vocabulary can become a quick and easy part of your daily routine once you make the effort to become consciously aware of words you hear and read. A 10-year-old reading for six minutes a day is exposed to about 430,000 words a year. If you become more attentive to the vocabulary and increase your recall by just 1 per cent, that's an extra 4,300 words in your brain tank each year.

Building your vocabulary will allow you to express yourself more clearly and fluently and the returns (social, psychological, financial) are their own reward. If you learned a new word each day for the next three years you would have over a thousand new words; if you spent five minutes a day learning five new words, you'd have over 18,000 within a decade.

Reading lots of books is a good way to keep existing vocabulary fresh in your mind, but you have to make a conscious effort if you want to learn new words: keep a dictionary close by to look up unfamiliar vocabulary, otherwise you will ignore the meaning and push on with the story.

Whenever you look up a new word, circle it in your dictionary with a red pen, so next time you open that page you can reread the word and its definition to consolidate it in your memory. Try also to consciously introduce recently learned words into your everyday writing and speech. Even when you hear someone use an unfamiliar word on the television, reach for that dictionary.

HOW MANY WORDS DO YOU KNOW?

To estimate the size of your own vocabulary, find a medium-sized dictionary, one which contains about 100,000 entries or 1,000 pages. Read 30 pages at random and make a tally of the number of words you recognize AND the number of words you understand (the former will be larger than the latter). Better still, check the definitions of the words you think you know because you may still be wrong! Finally, divide both totals by 30 and multiply by the total number of pages in your dictionary to discover how many words you recognize and know. It will probably be much higher than you think!

WHICH EIGHT OF THESE WORDS DO NOT EXIST?

(Look them all up in the dictionary and expand your vocabulary!)

abacinate	eleemosynary	flunge	lerret	testiculate
argand	enodate	fribble	lucubration	tribution
autolatrist	eructation	fugacious	perchery	utriform
callipygian	estivate	funambulist	quiddity	
delitescent	exultion	jentacular	scrutable	
despumate	fabiform	labrose	spiracle	

WORDSEARCH

The wordsearch puzzle contains 26 unusual words, each of which starts with a different letter of the alphabet.

```
W  R  B  I  B  B  L  E  T  H  O  L  O  G  I  C  A  D  N  N
L  S  U  O  H  C  I  R  T  O  L  U  U  M  M  E  V  N  R  Z
K  N  J  N  W  K  T  Z  G  Q  A  Y  P  E  P  G  E  I  V  I
E  N  W  Y  Y  B  Q  N  N  Q  Y  N  E  P  I  A  N  R  Q  E
J  M  N  C  A  V  P  C  U  R  B  Q  Q  T  G  T  T  G  S  T
T  V  X  H  K  R  M  E  T  D  D  Q  V  U  N  O  R  D  U  K
K  A  K  O  R  R  H  A  P  H  I  O  P  H  O  B  I  A  O  I
P  D  J  P  K  M  L  L  C  O  G  U  C  O  R  A  P  R  T  F
T  Q  R  H  C  O  A  O  A  R  N  W  S  C  A  C  O  G  N  R
Y  Z  H  A  I  J  G  F  E  S  O  Y  I  T  T  F  T  X  E  J
A  C  I  G  Y  P  O  T  A  E  T  S  T  D  E  A  E  F  M  I
P  X  A  Y  U  B  R  Q  J  X  I  R  M  T  D  R  N  E  U  F
V  H  B  G  G  O  D  H  C  W  O  E  O  A  I  I  T  R  J  Y
M  H  Y  S  I  A  R  D  M  U  N  B  C  B  T  T  F  I  B  T
X  I  I  T  M  R  H  O  T  N  E  U  Q  O  L  I  C  U  A  P
K  Z  I  V  I  T  A  P  B  Q  N  C  G  T  L  E  C  Q  L  N
Z  O  X  C  J  C  Y  P  O  R  H  T  N  A  O  Z  M  D  P  S
N  W  D  M  E  T  A  T  C  R  A  F  M  G  X  S  S  E  F  L
A  S  F  Q  X  P  I  M  D  W  E  Y  O  P  M  A  C  E  T  Y
U  Z  R  E  T  A  F  H  E  L  D  X  E  I  L  J  R  B  V  F
```

· ASTROBLEME · BIBBLE · CABOTAGE · DIGNOTION · EMACITY
· FARCTATE · GRADGRIND · HAGIOLATRY · IMPIGNORATE · JUMENTOUS
· KAKORRHAPHIOPHOBIA · LETHOLOGICA · MACROSMATIC · NUDIUSTERTIAN
· ONYCHOPHAGY · PAUCILOQUENT · QUIRE · RETROITION · STEATOPYGIC
· TITTYNOPE · ULOTRICHOUS · VENTRIPOTENT · WIDDIFUL · XEROPHAGY
· YARBOROUGH · ZOANTHROPY

WORD DEDUCTION

Match each word with its correct definition. In most cases you should be able to use your existing knowledge of common related words or word fragments to deduce the meanings.

hard scar tissue which grows over injured skin	tardiloquous
process of infection	macrotous
horse-drawn carriage with folding top	unguligrade
acorn-bearing	ranivorous
walking on hoofs	janitrix
winking	habilable
big-eared	widgeon
yellowish	landau
ten-line poem	vaticide
frog-eating	quadrilocular
pastoral or rustic poem	caducity
a straight bundle of straw used for thatching	sanative
birthmark	fabulist
killing of a prophet	octad
having shiny smooth scales	balaniferous
freshwater duck	decastich
slow in speech	xanthic
healing	yelm
to burn	eclogue
to blind using a red-hot metal plate	abacinate
set of eight things	ignify
a female janitor	ganoid
capable of being clothed	naevus
being of a transitory or impermanent nature	keloid
having four compartments	zymosis
one who invents fables	palpebration

SPEED READING

TRAINING YOURSELF TO SPEED READ MAY INVOLVE UNLEARNING SOME OF THE BAD HABITS YOU PICKED UP AS A CHILD. AS CHILDREN WE ARE TAUGHT THE ALPHABET, THEN WE PROGRESS ONTO WORDS AND PHRASES AND SENTENCES.

With practice our vocabulary grows and our speed and fluency increase but speed reading involves taking your attention away from individual words and phrases to take in bigger phrases, even whole sentences in one sweep of the eye. Anyone can learn to speed read without sacrificing comprehension. In fact, in many cases it increases comprehension.

An average reader reads about 200 words per minute with about 60 per cent comprehension; speed reading can boost your speed to over 1,000 words per minute with about 85 per cent comprehension. Here's how it works:

1. Before you begin, have a clear purpose for your reading and what information you want to absorb. Reading speed and efficiency are governed by motivation. Speed readers know what they want to achieve from the text. For instance, when reading a novel you look for story and character development and visualize descriptive passages, while a self-help book contains concepts, advice and instructions. If you establish what you're looking for, you know where to direct your attention.

2. Read silently. Don't even hear the words in your head, just read the words and let them flow into your thoughts. Subvocalization slows down your reading to a snail's pace because it makes you 'play' every single word, like practising scales on a piano. Speed reading is more like running the back of your thumb along the keyboard to play a glissando of thirty notes in less than a second.

3. You may have to hold the book/screen further away from your eyes to make a broad sweep with your eyes. Speed readers optimize the reading distance.

Experiment until you find the most effective and comfortable speed reading distance.

4. Skim quickly once for context to give you a framework on which to build the rest of your comprehension, then speed read for meaning.

5. Instead of reading individual words or phrases, darting your eyes back to reread certain words, keep your eyes moving forwards from left to right at a faster but constant speed. Only move your eyes back when you start a new line.

6. Run your finger along the line to force yourself to maintain a constant speed and to discourage you from 'regressing'. Eventually you should be able to move your hand away and simply run your eyes left and right along a *narrow band in the centre of the line*. While moving down the page, pick up the text on either side of the band with your peripheral vision.

7. Spot places where you can skim and scan. With practice you develop an intuition to recognize fillers, purple prose, repetition and recapping or heavily descriptive passages that are surplus to requirements (e.g. if you are reading a chapter of a thriller novel simply for plot development, you can skim over that three-paragraph description of a chill, damp, windy night until the story begins to move forward again).

8. Relax. When you are in the zone, speed reading feels smoother and easier than conventional reading and it is less tiring than slavishly paying attention to every single word. Relax your face, extend your gaze, let the words wash over you and you'll start to soak up blocks and sentences.

RIDDLES

Riddles have been around for thousands of years, appearing in many different cultures. One of the oldest riddles is 'The Riddle of the Sphinx' which comes from Greek mythology and has its earliest roots from about 470 BC. 'Which creature has one voice and yet becomes four-footed and two-footed and three-footed?' (answer on page 143).

The oldest known riddle is more than a thousand years older and appears on the famous Rhind Mathematical Papyrus, which was taken from the tomb of an ancient Egyptian scribe in the nineteenth century and today is kept in the British Museum in London. The papyrus contains 84 different mathematical problems including this:

In seven houses there are seven cats. Each cat catches seven mice. Each mouse would have eaten seven ears of corn and each ear of corn, if sown, would have produced seven hekats of grain. How many things are mentioned in total?

The answer is an astounding 19,607. There are seven houses, 49 cats (7 x 7), 343 mice (7 x 7 x 7), 2,401 ears of corn (7 x 7 x 7 x 7) and 16,807 hekats of grain (7 x 7 x 7 x 7 x 7).

7 + 49 + 343 + 2,401 + 16,807 = 19,607

EINSTEIN'S RIDDLE

Albert Einstein wrote this riddle during the nineteenth century. He said that 98 per cent of the world population would not be able to solve it (although he may have meant that only 2 per cent could solve it in their heads).

1. There are five houses, painted five different colours.

2. In each house lives a person of different nationality.

3. Each person drinks a different kind of beverage, smokes a different brand of cigarette and keeps a different pet.

1. The British man lives in a red house.

2. The Swede has a dog.

3. The Dane drinks tea.

4. The green house is just left of the white house.

5. The owner of the green house drinks coffee.

6. The Pall Mall smoker keeps birds.

7. The owner of the yellow house smokes Dunhill.

8. The man in the centre house drinks milk.

9. The Norwegian lives in the first house.

10. The man who smokes Blends lives next to the one who keeps cats.

11. The man who keeps horses lives next to the Dunhill smoker.

12. The man who smokes Blue Master drinks beer.

13. The German smokes Prince.

14. The Norwegian lives next to the blue house.

15. The Blend smoker's neighbour drinks water.

WHO OWNS THE FISH?

TWELVE RIDDLES

1. Three wise women are standing in a row facing forwards. Peri-banu is at the front, Soraya in the middle and Zeheratzade at the back. Each woman is wearing either a black or a white hat. They know that at least one hat is black and one hat is white but they don't know the colours of their own hats. Without speaking to each other or anyone else, how can one of the women work out the colour of her own hat?

2. Two men catch two fish in two minutes. At this rate, how many men could catch 500 fish in 500 minutes?

3. The more you take, the more you leave behind. What are they?

4. What goes up the chimney down, but can't go down the chimney up?

5. What has a foot but no legs?

6. I have a little house in which I live all alone. It has no doors or windows, and if I want to go out I must break through the wall. What am I?

7. There were five men going to church and it started to rain. The four that ran got wet and the one that kept still stayed dry. Why?

8. I fly but have no wings. I cry but have no eyes. I see the sky get dark and I see when the sun comes up. What am I?

9. Little trotty hetty coat, in a long petticoat, and a red nose – the longer she stands the shorter she grows. What is it?

10. It is in the rock, but not in the stone; It is in the marrow, but not in the bone; It is in the bolster, but not in the bed; It is not in the living, nor yet in the dead. What is it?

11. What walks all day on its head?

12. It's been around for millions of years, but it's no more than a month old. What is it?

DINGBAT PUZZLES ARE VISUAL WORD RIDDLES. THE BEST WAY TO SOLVE THEM IS TO SAY WHAT YOU SEE.

Draft

DR DR

NO NO CORRECT

All
All World All
All

PEEP

SGEG

MEAL MEAL MEAL MEAL

7953
WHELMING

DDDWESTDDD

1234
U

GOGOGO
GO
GO
GO
GO

ARMS
ARMS
UP
ARMS
ARMS

ALGEBRA AND THE
VANISHING CAMEL

Algebra as we know it today appeared at the end of the sixteenth century with the work of French mathematician François Viète. At its simplest, algebra is doing arithmetical calculations using non-numerical mathematical symbols, such as x, y and z.

The word 'algebra' comes from the Arabic word *Al-Jabr*, which first appeared in an Arabic treatise written in AD 820 by the Persian mathematician, Muhammad ibn Mūsā al-Khwārizmī, entitled *The Compendious Book on Calculation by Completion and Balancing*. The exact translation of *Al-Jabr* is unclear, but historians think it meant 'restoration' or 'completion', a reference to the technique of cancelling terms on opposite sides of the equals sign in an equation.

Before the sixteenth century the dominant algebra was the same system that had been developed in Persian Babylonia three thousand years earlier. Archaeologists have recovered clay tablets dating from 1800 to 1600 BC that express fractions, algebra, quadratic and cubic equations and even the Pythagorean theorem $a^2 + b^2 = c^2$. However, the algebra was what we now call 'rhetorical algebra' – written in full sentences, so for example, x + 1 = 2 would be 'The thing plus one equals two'.

The next development in algebraic expression was made in the third century AD by the acknowledged father of algebra, Diophantus of Alexandria, although most of his book *Arithmetica* does not survive today. His 'Diophantine equations' inspired seventeenth-century French lawyer and amateur mathematician Pierre de Fermat to propose his famous theorem (now known as Fermat's Last Theorem) that no three positive integers a, b and c can satisfy the equation $a^n + b^n = c^n$ for any integer value of n greater than two. He famously scribbled his conjecture in the margin of his copy of *Arithmetica* with the tantalizing boast that his proof was too big to fit on the page. Mathematicians spent the next 350 years trying to prove it.

SOLVE THESE PUZZLES USING ALGEBRA

For example, if we call the pumpkin x, the alarm clock y and the ice lolly z, we know that 3x + y = 110 and that 2x + 2y = 100. These are called simultaneous equations. If 3x + y = 110, then y = (110 - 3x). You can substitute (110 - 3x) for y in the second equation to find the value of x.

2x + 2(110 - 3x) = 100

2x + 220 - 6x = 100

-4x = 100 - 220

-4x = -120

x = 30

Now substitute 30 for x in one of the equations to find the value of y; then you can work out the value of z.

THE VANISHING CAMEL

A dying Sheikh summoned each of the princes in turn. To his eldest son he bequeathed half of his camels; his middle son received one third of his camels and his youngest son, one ninth of his camels. A servant was sent to count the camels. There were seventeen. Everyone scratched their heads, since there was no way that seventeen animals could be divided according to the Sheikh's wishes without chopping one of them into pieces. The Sheikh summoned the local mathematician who rode to the palace on his clapped-out old camel and immediately proposed a solution. What did he do?

NUMBER SEQUENCES

A number sequence is an ordered list of numbers in which the order is significant. The elements in a sequence form part or all of a countable set, such as the natural numbers. However, a sequence can be finite (e.g. counting from 1 to 20) or infinite (all positive odd integers: 1, 3, 5, 7 . . .).

There are several famous and important sequences in mathematics. The sequence of prime numbers (a natural number greater than 1 that can be divided, without a remainder, only by itself and by 1) which begins 2, 3, 5, 7, 11, 13, 17 . . . is an example of an infinite sequence (Euclid proved this 2,300 years ago). Primes become less frequent as the sequence progresses, so searching for them is a field of mathematics all by itself and large primes are essential for modern cryptology.

Another famous and beautiful infinite sequence is the Fibonacci Series 0, 1, 1, 2, 3, 5, 8, 13, 21, 34 . . . in which each number is the sum of the two previous numbers. This sequence is found frequently in nature from the spiral of a sea shell, the scales on a pineapple and the arrangement of petals on a flower to the pattern of florets in the core of a daisy blossom and the shoot growth of plants like the sneezewort.

To solve any polynomial sequence you use the method of 'finding the successive difference'.

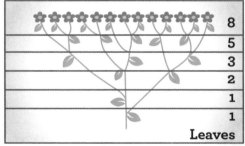

Suppose you have the sequence 3, 6, 11, 18 . . .

Write down the numbers in one row, then below them their differences, and then proceed writing successive differences:

Eventually you will reach a constant row (in this case it's 2 2 2). Now work backwards up the rows. You now know that the second row is formed by adding 2 to the previous number, so once you have 11, you can add it to the 27 in the top row to get the next in the sequence = 38.

SEQUENCE PUZZLES

1. In 1202, Italian mathematician Leonardo Fibonacci considered the question: how many pairs of rabbits can be produced from a single pair of newborn rabbits in one year if:

   • rabbits always produce one male and one female offspring

   • rabbits can reproduce once a month

   • each animal takes one month to reach breeding maturity

   • no rabbits die

   Hint: this puzzle can be solved using the Fibonacci Series to work out how many pairs of rabbits would exist at the beginning of each month.

   1 2 3 4 5 6 7 8 9 10 11 12 13

   1 1 2 3

2. What comes next in the sequence?

   a) 1, 4, 9, 16, 25, 36, 49, _____, _____

   b) 0, 1, 3, 6, 10, 15, _____, _____ (clue: • •⋰•)

   c) 1, 5, 12, 22, 35, _____, _____ (clue: ∘ ⬠)

   d) 1, 4, 27, 256, _____, _____

3. What is special about this finite number sequence?

   8, 4, 4, 9, 9, 7, 6, 3, 3, 2, 0

DO IMPOSSIBLE SUMS
IN YOUR HEAD

The key to mental arithmetic is recognizing ways to simplify the sums that you have to make and reducing the number of operations that you have to perform to reach the answer. There are scores of techniques including breaking down, halving or doubling numbers so you can use your times tables, to Vedic Maths, which is an entire system of methods that sometimes seem like magic tricks to the untrained observer. Use these techniques to make mental arithmetic easier.

1. Make a quick estimate so you know approximately where you're heading. For example, multiplying 25 x 52 is approximately 25 x 50 = 12.5 x 100 = 1,250. The exact answer is 1,300, which you could have reached by adding another (2 x 25). Alternatively, you may have spotted that 52 is the same as 13 x 4 (most people know this from playing cards). So the sum is 25 x 4 x 13 = 100 x 13 = 1,300.

2. When adding up a list of numbers, look for groups that make multiples of ten. For instance in this list 7+4+ 21+ 9 + 2+ 8 +36 you can group (2 +8) + (36 + 4) + (21 +9) + 7 = 10 + 40 + 30 + 7 = 87 which is an easier calculation than climbing to the answer by thinking 7, 11, 32, 41, 43, 51, 87.

3. Break down numbers into easier separate calculations.

    For example: 74 - 38 = 74 - 30 - 8 = 44 - 8 = 36.

4. When multiplying two large numbers, split them into factors, perform some of the larger sums that appear in your times tables (which everyone should know) and then multiply by the other factor, rounding up to a multiple of ten and then subtracting the multiple of the difference. Which sounds more complicated to explain than to perform:

    24 x 36 = 2 x (12 x 12) x 3 = 6 x 144 = 900 - 36 = 864

    16 x 14 = 2 x (8 x 7) x 2 = 4 x 56 = 200 + 24 = 224

5. Learn your 13th, 15th, 17th and 19th times tables. For example, this calculation is easy when you know that 4 x 17 = 68.

    36 x 68 = 3 x (12 x 17) x 4 = 12 x 204 = 2400 + 48 = 2,448

6. Vedic Maths offers an even quicker way to multiply ANY two 2-digit numbers, e.g. 46 x 82

Step 1

Multiply the numbers in the left-hand column (4 x 8 = 32)

$$\underline{4}6$$
$$= 32$$
$$\underline{8}2$$

Step 2

Multiply the diagonals and add the result (4 x 2) + (8 x 6) = 56

$$46$$
$$= 56$$
$$82$$

Step 3

Multiply the numbers in the right-hand column (6 x 2 = 12)

$$4\underline{6}$$
$$= 12$$
$$8\underline{2}$$

Step 4

Place the three results side by side 32 56 12 and if any of the results are two-digit numbers, working from left to right, add the left digit to the adjacent number (32 + 5)(6 + 1)2

Answer = 3,772.

This might seem complicated at first, but you will soon get the hang of it after practising a few sums on paper. Take your time. Go slowly to make sure you understand the principle. Check your answers with a calculator. Finally, when you are confident that you've cracked the method, put pen and paper to one side and start doing the four steps in your head. Visualizing the numbers, manipulating them diagonally and vertically and retaining three results in your head will have a powerful impact on your working memory.

SPOT THE RELATIONSHIP
BETWEEN NUMBERS

It's difficult to imagine life on earth before humans discovered numbers and it is certain that society, both ancient and modern, would scarcely function without them. However, something is even more powerful than the numbers themselves and that is the relationship between them. True power comes from manipulating numbers, combining them, abstracting them and understanding how other people use them to gain power, make money or create scientific miracles. This all boils down to an understanding of the relationship between numbers.

For example, do you know why David Beckham chose the number 23 for the back of his shirt at Real Madrid? A businessman and sports fan couldn't fail to spot that it's the same number that basketball legend Michael Jordan wore and consider that maybe Real Madrid were trying to cash in on a magic number in the sporting world. Marcus Du Sautoy, the Simonyi Professor for the Public Understanding of Science and a Professor of Mathematics at the University of Oxford, has made the same observation. In his book *The Number Mysteries*, he observes that 23 is a prime number and then proposes the novel theory that 'at the time of Beckham's move, all the Galácticos, the key players for Real Madrid, were playing in prime number shirts: Carlos . . . number 3; Zidane . . . number 5; Raul and Ronaldo . . . 7 and 11'. He muses, 'perhaps it was inevitable that Beckham got a prime number' and he cites a possible psychological advantage of playing a team of primes, based on his own experience of his Sunday league team being promoted after he persuaded the team to change its kit to primes.

These bizarre number relationships surround us; they are everywhere and they hove in sight with satisfying regularity once we begin to look out for them. In nature, one of the key relationships between numbers is the syncopated life cycles of animals and their predators. Du Sautoy describes an American species of cicada that hides underground and only surfaces every seventeen years, en masse, to breed and lay eggs. Then they all die, the next generation hatch and burrow underground where they remain for another seventeen years. Seventeen is a prime number, one that ensures that the breeding cycle of the cicada coincides with the life cycle of its main predator less frequently than if it emerged after an even number of years (*see* puzzle 1 on page 88). He concludes, 'as the cicadas discovered, knowing your maths is the key to survival in this world'.

What is the relationship between the numbers 8 and 27? At first, you might think, not very much. So let's look at the factors. The former has the factors 1, 2, 4 and 8; the second 1, 3, 9, 27.

Can you see a link yet? Have you noticed that both sets of factors are geometric sequences? So 2 x 2 x 2 = 8 and 3 x 3 x 3 = 27. So 8 and 27 can be represented as 2^3 and 3^3. So both numbers feature in the cube number sequence $u_n = n^3$ which looks like this: 1, 8, 27, 64, 125, 216 ... ($1^3, 2^3, 3^3, 4^3, 5^3, 6^3$ ...).

You can always find interesting and useful relationships between numbers although prime numbers are the most stubborn of numbers to give up their secrets. This explains why problems like the 'abc conjecture' remain some of the most important unsolved challenges in mathematics. Huge cash prizes are on offer to anyone who can solve them.

The more you tinker around under the hood of mathematics, the more connections you can make, the more beautiful, deep and ubiquitous these relationships become and the closer you edge towards winning a million dollars!

THE GOLDEN RATIO

Possibly the most fundamental relationship between numbers in nature and design is the golden ratio. Two numbers are in the golden ratio if their ratio is the same as the ratio of their sum to the larger of the two quantities.

The golden ratio (represented by the Greek letter 'phi' ɸ) is a special decimal fraction approximately equal to 1.618033. It appears many times in geometry, art, architecture and nature from the proportions of the Parthenon (the ancient Greek temple to Athena in Athens) and the *Mona Lisa* to the design of this Aston Martin.

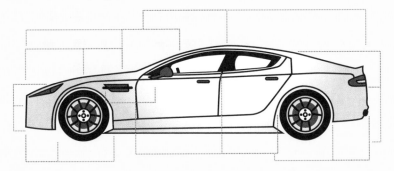

Most amazing of all, the golden ratio is synonymous with the Fibonacci Sequence 0, 1, 1, 2, 3, 5, 8, 13, 21, 34, 55, 89, 144 ... (*see* page 82). The further along the sequence we go, the closer the ratio between a number and its predecessor approaches 1.618.

In humans physical attraction is linked to phi. The more closely a face adheres to phi, the more attractive those traits are considered, since they are a potential indicator of reproductive fitness and health. Even our smiles can't escape the beautiful tyranny of the golden ratio. Studies have shown that the most attractive smiles are found in individuals whose central incisors are 1.618 times wider than the lateral incisors, which are 1.618 times wider than canines.

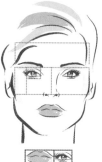

1. Suppose there were three species of subterranean cicadas. The blue cicada has a burrowing/breeding cycle of 7 years; the red cicada 12 and the yellow cicada 13 years. They share the same predator which emerges once every 8 years. All four species burrow underground in the year 1900, up to and including the year 2000:
   a) Which cicada will meet its predator four times?
   b) Which cicada will meet its predator once?
   c) Which cicada will never meet its predator?

2. What is the relationship between these two sequences?
   Hint: There are 25 prime numbers between 1 and 100, 4 in the first row and 5 in the first column.

   4, 4, 2, 2, 3, 2, 2, 3, 2, 1 and 5, 1, 7, 0, 1, 0, 6, 0, 5, 0

1	2	3	4	5	6	7	8	9	10
11	12	13	14	15	16	17	18	19	20
21	22	23	24	25	26	27	28	29	30
31	32	33	34	35	36	37	38	39	40
41	42	43	44	45	46	47	48	49	50
51	52	53	54	55	56	57	58	59	60
61	62	63	64	65	66	67	68	69	70
71	72	73	74	75	76	77	78	79	80
81	82	83	84	85	86	87	88	89	90
91	92	93	94	95	96	97	98	99	100

3. What is the relationship between 1597 and 2584?

PRIME NUMBERS AND
THE HUMAN BRAIN

In the previous section you were introduced to some of the curious properties of prime numbers, so now let's examine them in greater depth. A prime is a natural number greater than 1 that can be divided, without a remainder, only by itself and by 1. The sequence of primes begins 2, 3, 5, 7, 11, 13, 17, 19, 23, 29, 31 . . . and is an example of an infinite (though unpredictable) sequence.

Primes are indivisible numbers that are the building blocks of all other numbers. All other whole numbers can be factored down to their prime factors. For example, the building blocks (factors) of 64 are 1, 2, 4, 8, 16, 32 and 64 but the prime number 2 is the foundation of the other numbers: $2^2 = 4$, $2^3 = 8$, $2^4 = 16$, $2^5 = 32$ and $2^6 = 64$. Therefore 64 has just one prime factor (2) because 2 is the only number you need to build 64.

The factors of 510 are: 1, 2, 3, 5, 6, 10, 15, 17, 30, 34, 51, 85, 102, 170, 255, 510. But they can all be reduced down to the prime factors 2, 3, 5 and 17. Prime numbers truly are, in the words of Marcus Du Sautoy, 'the hydrogen and oxygen of the world of mathematics'. Prime numbers may even be the means by which we communicate with extra-terrestrials. In his science fiction novel, *Contact*, American astronomer, astrophysicist and cosmologist Carl Sagan explains in some detail how prime numbers could form the basis of a universal language, since primes exist independently of human language and thought.

THE SIEVE OF ERATOSTHENES

The third-century BC Greek mathematician Eratosthenes of Cyrene devised a quick method to find all the prime numbers up to 100. First write down all the numbers from 1 to 100. Cross out 1 (as shown in the example on page 90) because it is not a prime. Since 2 is the first prime, all multiples of 2 can't be prime, so circle them all in purple and move on to the next number, 3. Any multiples of 3 can't be prime, so you can circle them in green this time and move to the next uncircled number 5, etc. using a different colour each time. By the time you reach 11, all you are left with are uncircled primes.

This is one of the earliest recorded examples of an algorithm – a step-by-step procedure for solving a problem by applying a specific set of instructions (*see* page 92). It is still the most simple and effective method for locating the smaller primes (those less than, say, a million).

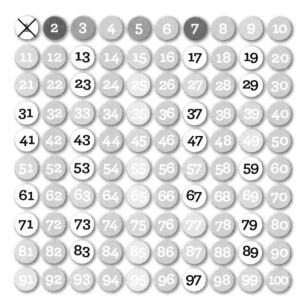

The first 100 numbers are awash with primes. There are 21 primes between 100 and 200, 16 primes between 200 and 300 and only 14 between 700 and 800. As you would expect, the primes get more scarce the further we count, because there are more factors.

PRIME PATTERNS

Some physicists believe that research into prime numbers will lead to a greater understanding of the complex computational apparatus of the human brain. The distribution of prime numbers is thought to be random, but quantum physics and probability theory are being used to try to discover if there is a hidden pattern among the smaller primes. Alexander Bershadskii from ICAR, Israel, explains the significance in his May 2011 open access article, 'Hidden Periodicity and Chaos in the Sequence of Prime Numbers':

'A physicist may ask: why should one be interested in finding these patterns? The answer is: comparison. If one can recognize patterns in an apparently random system, then one can compare these patterns with the patterns known for some other system of interest. We have already mentioned the comparison with certain quantum systems. Another intrinsic comparison can be made with the computational properties of brains, where the natural numbers certainly should play a crucial role. The neuron signals are also apparently random.

Can one compare patterns observed in these signals with the patterns in the prime numbers sequence in a constructive way, in order to shed a light on the computational apparatus of the brain?'

1. What are the smallest three prime numbers that can be written as a sum of the squares of two other prime numbers?

2. The first ten prime numbers are 2, 3, 5, 7, 11, 13, 17, 19, 23, 29.

    The prime factors of 30 (the number after 29) are 2, 3 and 5, so 30 is not a prime.

    30 + 1 = 31 which cannot be made by multiplying any of the previous prime numbers together, so it is a prime.

    Euclid used this elegant proof to show something fundamental about the set of prime numbers. What was it?

3. What's so special about the number 15,485,863?

THE AMAZING HALF DOZEN LEFTOVER TRICK

Ask a friend to pick any prime number bigger than 5 (but not to tell you).

Tell them to:

Square it (multiply the number by itself)

Add 17

Divide by 12

Without knowing which prime number was chosen, you can announce:

There will be a remainder of 6. Or if they do the sum on a calculator, the answer will end with '.5'

THE EQUALLY AMAZING TWO DOZEN TRICK

If you square any prime number bigger then 3, then subtract 1, the answer always divides by 24!

Try it with these prime numbers and see: 83, 277, 2,707, 6,053, 17,449.

ALGORITHMS AND
ARTIFICIAL INTELLIGENCE

An algorithm is a step-by-step procedure for solving a problem by applying a specific set of instructions. We programme computers using algorithms. We write computer software that gives the computer a series of steps and it completes them with blistering speed. The earliest computers worked on the same principle, except that the mechanism consisted of metal wheels, gears and cogs, instead of zeros and ones. The operator set up the initial conditions and then the mechanical computer would crunch through a series of predetermined operations to reach the inevitable result.

The earliest known mechanical computer is over 2,000 years old. The Antikythera Mechanism was discovered in 1901 by six sponge divers off the coast of Crete. It was on the ocean floor among the remains of a ship that had sunk in 76 BC. The device was originally constructed using 32 interlocking bronze gears fitted inside a wooden case and is thought to be an astronomical calculator.

The main difference between this extraordinary artefact and modern computers is the speed at which they can perform calculations, but they can only work if we tell them what to do – by giving them algorithms.

COMPUTERS AND THE HUMAN BRAIN

We created computers, so it isn't surprising that their operation is governed by our metacognition (understanding of thinking), logic and mathematics, but recent research has revealed that there is a link between how a computer 'learns' using recurrent neural networks (RNNs) and algorithms, and how our brains function while we sleep.

One of the earliest RNNs, a Boltzmann machine, was invented in 1985 by AI pioneers, Geoffrey Hinton and Terry Sejnowski. It is 'stochastic' which means it introduces *random variations* into the network. A Boltzmann machine starts with a random distribution of 'weight' within its network. It is then 'trained' by being fed data, one layer at a time; weights are then tweaked to reinforce the observed response inside the network. This observation is made by comparing the firing pattern of the nodes within the network with the random baseline pattern when the machine is not being fed data. Over time, meaningful relationships between nodes are gradually established and reinforced by this weight tweaking.

Ten years after he co-created the Boltzmann machine, Hinton proposed a theory that sleep 'serves the same function as the baseline component of the algorithm, the rate of neural activity in the absence of input' (*Quanta Magazine*, Natalie Wolchover). The brain relies on sleep to figure out which neural connections need to be reinforced, which is why sleep is essential for memory consolidation. 'You're figuring out how correlated would these neurons be if the system were running by itself. And then if the neurons are more correlated than that, increase the weight between them. And if they're less correlated than that, decrease the weight between them.'

ALGORITHMIC MAGIC TRICK

This trick works well with two or three people at the same time. It relies on the golden ratio (*see* page 87) and a simple algorithm.

1. Give your subject a calculator and a pen and paper and ask them to write down two whole numbers between 1 and 50 (but not tell you).

2. Ask them to add the two numbers.

3. They now have three numbers. Ask them to add the two larger numbers.

4. Repeat at least another eight times (add the largest two numbers each time).

5. Ask them to tell you the highest number and then tell them to add the two largest numbers one final time.

6. While they are doing this, you can predict what their final number is by performing this simple algorithm: MULTIPLY THE NUMBER THEY TOLD YOU BY 1.61803398 (this is the golden ratio) and then round up or down to the nearest whole number.

For example if they chose 13 and 45, steps would appear like this:

13 + 45 = 58

45 + 58 = 103

58 + 103 = 161

103 + 161 = 264

161 + 264 = 425

264 + 425 = 689

425 + 689 = 1,114

689 + 1,114 = 1,803

1,114 + 1,803 = 2,917

1,803 + 2,917 = **4,720** (this is the number they give you)

2,917 + 4,720 = **7,637** (while they work this out, you multiply 4,720 by 1.61803398 = 7,637.1203 = **7,637** to the nearest whole number)

HOW TO CALCULATE THE SQUARE
OF SEVEN AND A HALF IN YOUR HEAD

Here's the algorithm: $n^2 - (n - 0.5)^2 + (n - 0.25)$

That looks complicated but all it means is to find 7.5 squared, subtract the half to get 7, square this (to get 49), then add 7.25 = 56.25

This works for ANY number that ends in a half so:

to find 9.5 squared, subtract the half to get 9, square this (to get 81), then add 9.25 = 90.25

to find 23.5 squared, subtract the half to get 23, square this (to get 529), then add 23.25 = 552.25

VISUAL DISCRIMINATION

VISUAL DISCRIMINATION IS THE ABILITY
TO DISTINGUISH THE DIFFERENCES AND
SIMILARITIES IN SHAPES, FORMS, COLOURS,
SIZES, POSITIONS AND ORIENTATIONS.

We constantly use our sight to compare the features of different items and to tell items apart. Without this ability we wouldn't be able to read, write, recognize our friends, cook a meal, drive a car or even brush our teeth. Individuals can develop this skill, but most of us already enjoy a high level of visual discrimination that we take for granted.

The most important brain area involved in this ability is the occipital lobe, at the back of the skull. Face recognition is a specific aspect of visual discrimination associated with a part of the temporal lobe and occipital lobe called the fusiform gyrus. Facial recognition disorders such as acquired prosopagnosia (also known as face blindness) are often the result of occipito-temporal lobe damage.

The eponymous 'Man Who Mistook His Wife for a Hat' in Oliver Sacks' famous case study of brain function problems, suffered from a visual discrimination disorder called agnosia. He was a highly erudite and talented musician who not only failed to see faces but 'saw faces when there were no faces to see' and 'when in the street he might pat the heads of water hydrants and parking meters, taking these to be the heads of children'. He relied on individual details to recognize people, such as an item of clothing, the sound of their voice, the colour of their nail varnish or a distinctive moustache. Sacks describes how at the end of the consultation the man, 'reached out his hand and took hold of his wife's head, tried to lift it off, to put it on. He had apparently mistaken his wife for a hat! His wife looked as if she was used to such things.'

1. SPOT THE DIFFERENCES PUZZLE

Find ten differences between the two beach scenes.

2. SHAPE MATCHING

Which red and yellow shapes match exactly
(apart from having been flipped, rotated or both)?

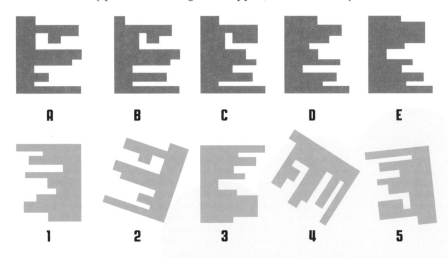

3. CRIME SCENE

Five fingerprints discovered at a crime scene were tested against ten fingerprints on the
police database. How many of the lifted prints can you match with the database?

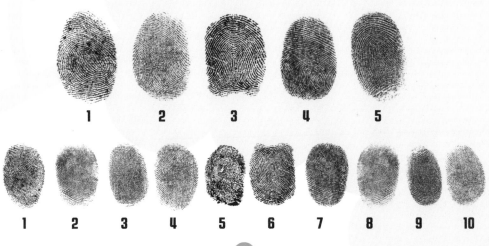

CONTRAST DISCRIMINATION

This is one aspect of our visual discrimination that is ripe for duping; designers of illusions often exploit contrast to fool the viewer's perception.

In 1935, Gestalt psychologist Kurt Koffka described this simultaneous contrast illusion (now known as the Koffka Ring Illusion). A grey ring on a light and dark background appears uniform, but when the halves are slid apart vertically, the two halves of the ring appear to be different shades of grey. If the rings are intertwined the effect is even more startling.

1. Are the three centre squares the same or different colours?

2. Which red circle is the bigger?

THE CHARPENTIER SIZE–WEIGHT ILLUSION

Prepare two boxes, one large and one small. Tape a full one-litre plastic bottle to the bottom of each box so it can't roll around. Close the lids and place the boxes on the floor. Ask a volunteer to lift each box in turn and decide which is the heavier.

Which box do you think they will choose? Maybe the bigger one, because it looks heavier? Actually, the opposite is true. Repeated tests have shown that subjects report the smaller box to be the heavier.

The Charpentier Illusion was first published in 1891 by French physician Augustin Charpentier but we still don't fully understand why it works. Charpentier discovered that if you place identical weights inside closed boxes of differing sizes and then lift the boxes, the smaller box will always feel heavier than the bigger one.

Until recently, the traditional explanation was that when you pick up the bigger box, you overcompensate for its size and put too much effort into lifting. This makes the larger box appear lighter than it really is, so you judge the smaller box to be heavier.

However, in 2000 this theory was disproved by Professor Randy Flanagan and his student, Mike Bletzner, at Queen's University, Ontario, Canada. They allowed subjects to alternatively lift both boxes so that they could correctly judge the force required in each case. Even after they had become accustomed to using the correct amount of lifting force and were TOLD that both boxes weighed the same, subjects still judged the smaller weighted box to be heavier. In a related experiment, subjects reported the same even when the smaller box was made lighter.

The illusion is one of visual perception rather than leverage or people using a different stance to lift the bigger box. This has been proved because the illusion also works with boxes that differ only in their construction material (rather than size). Metal containers feel lighter than wooden containers of the same size and mass; darker objects feel lighter than brighter objects of the same size and mass.

VISUAL MEMORY

Visual memory is a vitally important perceptual and learning skill. It is the ability to store visual sensations and perceptions when the stimuli that prompted them have been removed. Research suggests that in sighted people, 80 per cent of learning relies on the eyes; visual memory and the ability to form and retain mental images are key components of learning.

Information remains in our visual memory for a very short time, approximately several hundred milliseconds, shorter than auditory memory which lasts for a few seconds and can be retained indefinitely with repetition (e.g. when someone tells us a phone number, we can repeat it to ourselves until we find pen and paper to write it down).

When we perform a visual memory test like the one on the next page, most of us do not rely on short-term photographic recall alone; we have to think about what we are seeing, pay attention and internally verbalize to interpret and store the visual data (e.g. I can see two oranges, a mug, a blue pen, a book). Very few people can close their eyes and scan the visual image in their minds as if it were still there. However, the ability to recall images in great detail for several minutes is more common in childhood. Between 2 and 10 per cent of children have this skill but it seems to diminish after the age of six, probably because language and auditory memory become dominant.

Some individuals, such as the autistic savant Stephen Wiltshire, have eidetic memory and can recall visual information apparently indefinitely and in minute and accurate detail. Wiltshire draws detailed pen and ink drawings of cityscapes from memory. He drew a 10-metre-long panorama of Manhattan after a short helicopter ride, although even he appears to 'think' about what he views, rather than just blink his eyes and take a mental photograph. He says, 'When I am drawing I am thinking about the information and the details so I can memorize it and then draw it back.' He is passionate about cities, so he is emotionally engaged and highly motivated to remember what he sees, which is another important memory component.

Study the picture for one minute. Look at it carefully and try to remember as many details as possible. After the minute is up, turn the page and answer the questions.

1. How many pairs of shoes are there?

2. What colour are the towels?

3. What is directly below the black sunglasses?

4. What is inside the basket?

5. What colours are the two telephones?

6. On the top row, which direction does the hook of the coat hanger point, left or right?

7. On which horizontal row was the globe?

8. Which continent is visible on the globe, America or Africa?

9. At the top left is a pile of how many pairs of jeans?

10. What is below the red shirt?

11. Do the blue stripes on the blue shirt go from top left to bottom right or from top right to bottom left?

12. Which two objects below are NOT in the picture?

13. Does the light bulb have a screw or bayonet fitting?

14. What colour is the little label inside the waistband of the blue jeans?

15. How many piles of newspapers are there?

16. What colour is the sand in the egg timer?

17. What are the headphones resting on?

18. What colour is the hairbrush?

19. The solitary training shoe fits which foot, left or right?

20. What colour is the lace on this shoe?

FIGURE GROUND

Figure ground is the perceptual skill that enables us to pick out objects from their background or surrounding images. We recognize shapes and can distinguish them because of their form or silhouette, even when presented with a visually complex scene. Form, silhouette or shape are naturally perceived as figure (object), while the surrounding area is perceived as ground (surroundings/background).

'Hidden picture' puzzles and specific types of visual illusions work by creating an ambiguous relationship between figure and ground, so that one image hides within another, or figure and ground merge or swap places.

One of the most famous figure-ground illusions is the so-called 'Boring figure' which is named after the man who brought it to public attention, the experimental psychologist Edwin Boring, who was born in 1886 in Philadelphia, Pennsylvania. The image was drawn by cartoonist W. E. Hill and is entitled *My Wife and My Mother-in-Law*. The image can be viewed either as a beautiful young woman or an old lady wearing a head scarf (the chin and left ear of the young woman are the nose and left eye of the old lady respectively).

Another famous figure-ground illusion is Rubin's vase, created around 1915 by the Danish psychologist Edgar Rubin. Rubin explains: 'When two fields have a common border, and one is seen as figure and the other as ground, the immediate perceptual experience is characterized by a shaping effect which emerges from the common border of the fields and which operates only on one field or operates more strongly on one than on the other.'

Figure ground features in one of the six principles of Gestalt – a theory of visual perception developed by German psychologists in the 1920s. Gestalt means 'unified whole' and works on the basis that people tend to organize visual stimuli into groups, every stimulus is perceived in its simplest form and the whole is greater than the sum of its parts. The Gestalt principle of area states that the smaller of two overlapping figures is perceived as figure while the larger is regarded as ground.

Another artist who played with figure and ground was the sixteenth-century Italian painter Giuseppe Arcimboldo, who painted portrait heads made out of fruit, vegetables, flowers and a variety of other objects.

During the twentieth century, Dutch graphic artist M. C. Escher produced many woodcuts, lithographs and mezzotints depicting positive-negative geometric shapes (*Day and Night*, 1938) or flocks of tessellated birds transforming into fish.

The dream architecture of Surrealists such as Salvador Dalí also included illusions which manipulate the figure-ground relationship. *The Invisible Man* (1929), the first painting in which Dalí used double images, *Apparition of Face and Fruit Dish on a Beach* (1938) and *Slave Market with the Disappearing Bust of Voltaire* (1940) are prime examples of this technique.

Recently even the notoriously ambiguous *Mona Lisa* has come under renewed scrutiny after artist Ron Piccirillo found the heads of a lion, an ape and a buffalo in the background after turning the painting on its side. His discovery and references in da Vinci's journals have convinced Piccirillo that the painting is a depiction of envy.

Contemporary branding design often exploits the figure-ground relationship. For example, the corporate logo of FedEx has a white arrow hidden within the orange 'Ex'; a negative space in the middle of the Formula One logo creates the '1', of which the viewer only becomes aware when it shifts in perception from ground to figure (it's also an example of visual closure – see page 107).

Figure-ground manipulation isn't just restricted to the art world. Camouflage is visually disruptive because it breaks up contour and silhouette, so figure and ground blend together. There are examples throughout the animal kingdom of species that have evolved to resemble their surroundings and military camouflage exploits the same principle of disrupting the relationship between figure and ground.

How many of the objects below can you find hidden in the picture?

1. The first rectangle contains a 6-sided hexagon. Which of the figures that follow also contain a 6-sided figure?

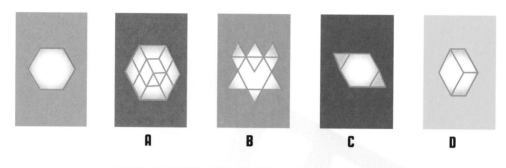

A   B   C   D

2. Can you spot these shapes within the pattern?

A   B   C   D   E   F   G

VISUAL CLOSURE

Visual closure is the ability to visualize a complete whole from incomplete information or a partial picture. It is the visual equivalent of the inductive reasoning discussed on page 32. This skill enables us to quickly form a 'Gestalt' understanding of objects and the visual environment even when details are missing. It is a foundation skill for fluency and speed in reading and spelling. When we first learn to read, our eyes fix on one word at a time, but as we become faster and more proficient, they fix less often so we only perceive a part of a word and our brain fills in the rest.

Visual closure features in one of the six principles of Gestalt (*see* page 104). It enables you to read these words, even though part of the letters have been erased:

You can also recognize this animal and figure out that this picture fragment is from a car: and if you are very skilled, you might even recognize it as a Porsche.

Closure also makes us perceive shapes in negative space, like the cube, triangle and 3-D sphere:

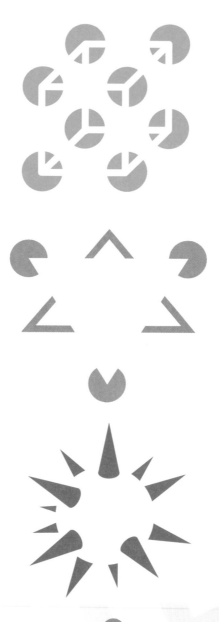

CAN YOU NAME THESE FAMOUS LANDMARKS?

NEAR–FAR
FOCUS SHIFTS

In people with normal healthy eyesight, about 70 per cent of eye focusing is performed by the cornea, the transparent front part of the eye that covers the iris and pupil. Behind the cornea is a layer of aqueous fluid and then a second lens system. The ciliary muscles in the eye change the shape of the crystalline lens by stretching it at the edges, to focus light rays onto the retina, the light-sensitive region at the back of the eye.

The ciliary muscles are relaxed when we gaze into the distance, but they have to work hard to achieve near focus. The efficiency of a person's near and far focus depends on the strength and flexibility of the eye muscles. People can experience eye focusing problems for a variety of reasons, but eye strain and tense, rigid ciliary muscles make it harder for them to change the lens to the required shape, so vision becomes blurred. Other factors that affect the eye muscle are loss of flexibility due to ageing (a condition called presbyopia, which also involves a loss of elasticity of the crystalline lens, causing the need for bifocals and/or reading glasses), poor diet, lack of exercise, smoking and alcohol abuse.

Extended periods of close-focus work, such as reading, working on a computer or texting, can also cause eye muscle tension. You may have noticed how looking at a computer screen or mobile phone for an extended period can make your far focus blurred when you take a break and look out of the window. This is because your eye muscles become strained and cannot perform near–far focus shift quickly enough. When doing near-focus work it is important to take regular breaks and to shift your focus into the distance. Your eye muscles relax when you look at something far away (which is one of the reasons why staring at the horizon or at a landscape is so refreshing).

Another sign of eye strain is over-focusing for close work (accommodative spasm); your eyes feel jittery and uncomfortable when you focus on fine print or work in dim light. Fortunately, you can improve the relaxation and flexibility of your eye muscles with this simple exercise to help you perform near–far focus shifts more easily. If you have eye strain and your vision is blurred on close-up reading, far-focus reading, or both, practise this exercise daily to improve your vision and to relax your eyes.

1	2	3	4	5
6	7	8	9	10
11	12	13	14	15
16	17	18	19	20
21	22	23	24	25
26	27	28	29	30

1. Hang a page a month wall calendar on the wall and sit down facing the wall about 3 m (10 ft) away from it.

2. Hold this book about 15 cm (6 in) from your eyes and focus on the number 1. If it is too blurry, move the book further away to help you to focus.

3. Once the 1 on the page is sharply in focus, shift your attention to the wall calendar and focus on the 1 on the calendar. Keep concentrating until the number is sharply in focus.

4. Now move your eyes back to the page and focus on the number 2. When it is sharply in focus, switch your attention to the number 2 on the wall calendar.

5. Repeat this process with every number of the month.

6. If you completed the task with ease, try again, only this time hold the book a little closer to your face so that your eyes have to work harder for near focus. With daily practice you should be able to perform the exercise while holding the book 8–10 cm (3½–4 in) away from your eyes and still maintain efficient near–far focus.

ACROSTICS

An acrostic is a form of writing, usually a poem, in which the initial, final or other chosen letter of each line, sentence or paragraph spells out a hidden word or message. The word 'acrostic' comes from combining the Greek words ἄκρος (extreme) and στίχος (line/verse). Acrostics can be used for encryption or as powerful mnemonics (devices to aid memory retrieval); they are a great way to invent passwords you'll never forget (because you've already learned them).

The Greeks of the Alexandrine period, the poets of the Italian Renaissance and the Elizabethans were fond of acrostics. The first printed version of an acrostic poem is 'The Strife of Love in a Dream', written at the end of the fifteenth century by a lovelorn monk who was unable to express his romantic feelings any other way. The initial letters of the first words of each section spell out, in Latin, the message, 'Brother Francis Colonna passionately loves Polia'.

Acrostics are one of the many interesting rhetorical features of the Hebrew Bible and the Greek exclamation 'Ἰησοῦς Χριστός, Θεοῦ Υἱός, Σωτήρ; Iesous CHristos, THeou Yios, Soter' (Jesus Christ, son of God, saviour) spells out ICHTHYS (ΙΧΘΥΣ), Greek for fish, which was used by early Christians as a secret symbol to avoid persecution.

In the early seventeenth century, when it was common practice for authors to remain anonymous to avoid incurring the wrath of the king or other powerful factions, a history book about Henry VIII, Edward VI and Queen Mary, entitled *Rerum Anglicarum Henrico VIII, Eduardo VI et Maria Regnantibus Annales,* was published anonymously and its author escaped detection until after his death. The acrostic 'Bishop Francis Godwin, Bishop of Llandaff, wrote these lines' was spelled out by the initial letter of each chapter.

Acrostics are a brilliant way to store scores of passwords by taking the initial or final letters of words of a song which you already know. For instance, this password was created by taking the initial letters of words in the first two lines of a famous Elvis Presley hit: *twtapitcjtpbwtatbtw*

It's 'Jailhouse Rock'. The great thing about acrostic passwords is that all you have to remember is the song title, so even if you forget the words you can look them up. If you want to keep a note of your passwords, you can create a playlist in your mp3 player, or write a list of songs in a Word document; if anyone finds them they won't know that they are passwords.

A VALENTINE

by Edgar Allan Poe (published 1846)

For her this rhyme is penned, whose luminous eyes,
  Brightly expressive as the twins of Lœda,
Shall find her own sweet name, that, nestling lies
  Upon the page, enwrapped from every reader.
Search narrowly the lines! – they hold a treasure
  Divine – a talisman – an amulet
That must be worn at heart. Search well the measure –
  The words – the syllables! Do not forget
The trivialest point, or you may lose your labor!
  And yet there is in this no Gordian knot
Which one might not undo without a sabre,
  If one could merely comprehend the plot.
Enwritten upon the leaf where now are peering
  Eyes scintillating soul, there lie perdus
Three eloquent words oft uttered in the hearing
  Of poets, by poets – as the name is a poet's, too.
Its letters, although naturally lying
  Like the knight Pinto – Mendez Ferdinando –
Still form a synonym for Truth. – Cease trying!
  You will not read the riddle, though you do the best you can do.

Poe wrote this poem for a specific person.
The woman's name is hidden within the text – can you find it?

ACROSTIC PASSWORDS

Here is a list of twelve initial letter acrostic passwords; see if you can crack them.
The only clues are the musical genres.

tcisMbTjab (Blues)

afiwaiwp (Disco)

sihtbawgayltjom (Country)

dpmcictte (Hip Hop)

talwsatgig (Rock)

olohlgtafar (Reggae)

eoppcaIysosd (Heavy Metal)

owspospwv (Punk)

lbothlbmott (Folk)

sitmsibswtec (Soul)

ijcgyoomhbyliaita (Pop)

ipmdtatidmsbcnc (Power Ballad)

HISTORY OF THE ACROSTIC PUZZLE

During the nineteenth century, acrostic poetry morphed into word puzzles. England's Queen Victoria was a known fan and even composed her own acrostic puzzles, so she may have helped to make them fashionable. Can you solve one of her double acrostics? When the correct answers are filled in, two separate acrostics will be revealed, reading down the first line and up the second.

A city in Italy (6) □ _ _ _ _ □

A river in Germany (4) □ _ _ □

A town in the US (10) □ _ _ _ _ _ _ _ _ □

A town in North America (10) □ _ _ _ _ _ _ _ _ □

A town in Holland (9) □ _ _ _ _ _ _ _ □

The Turkish name of Constantinople (8) □ _ _ _ _ _ _ □

A town in Bothnia (6) □ _ _ _ _ □

A city in Greece (7) □ _ _ _ _ _ □

A circle on the globe (8) □ _ _ _ _ _ _ □

MEMORY PEG

Memory peg is a mnemonic technique which involves hanging the information you want to commit to memory on visual number pegs. It's an effective way to remember a group of items such as a shopping list, and in a specific order.

Before you begin, you must choose a memorable image for each numeral from 1 to 10 that closely resembles the written form. This converts the abstract data into a more memorable visual form, which you can then use as memory pegs to associate with the other items that you want to commit to memory. Once established, your same ten number images can be used for every subsequent memory peg list. Here are some examples, but feel free to devise your own:

1 = *candle*　**2** = *swan*　**3** = *heart*　**4** = *sail of a yacht*　**5** = *hook*

6 = *elephant's trunk*　**7** = *axe*　**8** = *hourglass*　**9** = *balloon on a string*　**10** = *doughnut*

Take each item on your shopping list and bond it to a number image to tell a story or create an unforgettable scene, the more imaginative the better. To recall the items, simply run through each number image (candle, swan, heart, etc.) and the linked item on your shopping list (milk, bananas, bagels) will appear in your mind.

1. **Milk:** white candle melting off the table and all over the floor (like spilt milk)

2. **Bananas:** a swan riding a giant inflatable banana

3. **Bagels:** a toasted bagel on a bright pink, heart-shaped plate

4. **Orange juice:** a huge orange sailing in a yacht in a bright orange sea

5. **Tin of tomatoes:** opening a tin of tomatoes with a huge meat hook

6. **Yogurt:** an elephant sneezes loudly and showers you with yogurt

7. **Biscuits:** opening a packet of your favourite biscuits with an axe

8. **Red peppers:** an hourglass made out of peppers

9. **Onions:** a clown holding a heavy onion balloon, crying

10. **Chocolate:** a huge pile of doughnuts covered in runny chocolate

THE TOP 10 WOMEN'S TENNIS PLAYERS OF ALL TIME

1. Martina Navratilova
2. Steffi Graf
3. Chris Evert
4. Margaret Court
5. Serena Williams
6. Billie Jean King
7. Monica Seles
8. Venus Williams
9. Evonne Goolagong
10. Justine Henin

Simply link each player with a number image, or if you aren't a tennis fan and these people are just names to you, then you'll also need to devise a familiar image to help you recall the name or part of the name:

1. **Martina Navratilova:** A **rat** dressed in a sailor's outfit (**navy rat**) gives Chris **Martin** (from Coldplay) a **candle**
2. **Steffi Graf:** A **swan** points at a **graph** and won't let you go upstairs until you pay a **stair fee**
3. **Chris Evert:** **Chris** Rock does **a fart** on a **heart** cushion

ONCE UPON A PEG

Imagine you had to memorize the Twelve Labours of Hercules in the correct order: Nemean lion, Lernaean hydra, Ceryneian hind, Erymanthian boar, etc.

On your own or with a friend, concoct an imaginative, crazy and funny story involving your number images and auditory prompts to help you remember each item in the list. You might begin, 'Once upon a peg, a **mean** old **lion** set fire to his mane with a **candle**, while he was helping a **swan** search for her **learn**er's permit in a **high drawer** during a power cut, **carrying a knee** be**hind** his **heart,** when a **hairy man pour**ed water on his **sail** . . .' At any time your friend can challenge you to explain your tortured associations; this way you can compete for the most imaginative and ridiculous story elements, helping you both to build multiple associations to reinforce information as well as the sequence in which they occur.

Also, linking items with number images means that you can retrieve individual items without having to go through the whole story.

MEMORY PALACE

We have seen in the previous section that memory and recall are enhanced by using visual imagery, especially with abstract data. The memory palace (also known as 'method of loci') also uses visual imagery, but it ties objects to specific places and the story is replaced by a mental journey from one item to another.

Many professional memory champions claim to use this technique to remember lists of words, numbers, playing cards, faces and names. The system is actually more than 2,000 years old: it first appears in ancient Roman and Greek writings, including the anonymous *Rhetorica ad Herennium*, Cicero's *De Oratore* and Quintilian's *Institutio Oratoria,* which all date back to the first century BC. In these ancient societies public speakers were expected to remember their speeches, using notes was frowned upon and they didn't have PowerPoint presentations to jog their memories, so the method of loci was very popular.

As the name suggests (*loci* is the plural of *locus,* the Latin for place), it involves placing the objects that you want to memorize at specific locations within a familiar environment such as a building, cityscape or landscape. To memorize and recall the items you mentally walk through the environment using a predetermined route so that you can recall them in order.

Brain scans of professional memorizers who use the method of loci technique have shown activity in areas of the brain linked to spatial awareness, including the medial parietal cortex, retrosplenial cortex and the right posterior hippocampus.

In the recent BBC series, Sherlock Holmes uses his 'memory palace' to retrieve information and in one of the episodes blackmailer Charles Augustus Magnussen uses the loci method to store immeasurable amounts of blackmail data.

MEMORY EXERCISE 1

Choose the interior of a building that you know very well and can clearly visualize. Here are the first twelve items from the visual memory test on page 101:

Mentally walk around the building and working from the top left, go along the row and mentally place each object in a specific part of the environment. You could choose a separate room for each item, or you may be able to place all twelve at definite locations within a single room. Always walk either clockwise or anticlockwise around each room – whichever feels most natural to you. To root each item in a specific spot, make it interact in some way with the existing items in the room. To recall your items you must retrace your steps and perform the exact same journey.

MEMORY EXERCISE 2

To memorize a to-do list, use the same journey, only this time choose features on the list and make these interact with the environment. For example, you want to remember 'buy dog food' and the kettle area in your kitchen is one of your locations. So you might imagine a big pile of dog food dumped on top of the kettle – and maybe even throw the dog into this scenario, on top of the work surface, gobbling up all the food, tail wagging. The more imaginative and detailed your visual image, the easier it will be to recall. In a week's time, you'll still be able to remember this dog food example.

You might expect the items from both memory exercises to interfere with each other but this shouldn't be a problem, because even though you add new items to each locus, the context of each separate group of items helps to bind them together, so you can work out which item fits each list. However, you should avoid using the same journey for similar lists (such as two lots of shopping).

MULTISENSORY INPUT

Research has proved a link between engaging the senses of touch, taste, sight, hearing and smell and memory retention and recall. We have all experienced a smell that takes us back to childhood or a piece of music that evokes powerful emotion from our past or a specific event. Memories are formed and consolidated best when they engage many senses.

There is also an important emotional component, which is why time seems to stand still during an emergency, because in this heightened emotional state we actually create more memories. Our most vivid autobiographical memories tend to be of emotional events. Scientists have even heightened memory retention by artificially inducing unpleasant physical or emotional stimuli.

A recent study involving 322 subjects at Georgia Institute of Technology (Georgia Tech) called 'Evaluating the Importance of Multisensory Input on Memory and the Sense of Presence in Virtual Environments' showed that 'in particular, the addition of tactile, olfactory and auditory cues to a virtual environment increased the user's sense of presence and memory of the environment. Surprisingly, increasing the level of visual detail did not result in an increase in the user's sense of presence or memory of the environment.'

Teachers have long known that messy play – sticky, slippery, gooey 'hands-on' experiences with materials – reinforces learning by involving multiple senses. So the best way to learn is to introduce an emotional component into the experience and engage as many of your senses as possible, not just your sight.

Turn to page 101 and repeat the memory exercise, only this time, imagine the taste, smells, sounds and textures of the objects. Because this is your second attempt, you will find it easier, but notice which objects are the easiest to remember when you involve all your senses. For example, imagine licking the bone-dry towel (goosebumps!); recall the starchy-soapy smell of new jeans; press your open palm into the hairbrush; run your fingers along the contours of the basket.

REMEMBER
NAMES AND FACES

Humans are programmed to remember faces. In 1971, the scientists Goldstein and Chance showed subjects photographs of faces, magnified snowflakes and ink blots and discovered that the faces were most easily recalled, followed by the ink blots and the snowflakes.

The science supports the anecdotal evidence: most of us don't have any trouble recalling a face (although as many as 2.5 per cent of the population suffer from prosopagnosia – genetic face blindness); it's the name that is meant to go with it that causes us so many problems.

Forgetting a name isn't just embarrassing; it can harm your relationships and your career. We all think we are more memorable than the average person, so when someone forgets your name it can feel like a personal slight, even when you can't remember theirs.

The most important brain area involved in facial recognition is a region called the fusiform face area (FFA), which runs along the underside of the temporal and occipital lobes. Like most brain functions, it develops with practice and becomes specialized as we grow older. Babies can recognize faces long before they can talk, but they particularly become specialized to recognize human faces and they further specialize within the racial groups to which they are exposed. So just as the ability to learn foreign languages like a native drops off in infancy, recognizing faces from other ethnic groups also declines without regular exposure.

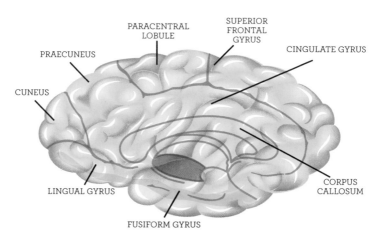

Facial recognition also has a strong emotional component. Face-processing brain areas interact with emotional memory networks, so when we see a face we can recall how we feel about that person and assess whether they are an ally or a threat; family or stranger. When this complex emotional-facial memory malfunctions, individuals develop Capgras syndrome, the delusion that loved ones have been replaced by identical-looking impostors.

1. When you meet someone for the first time, make sure you listen to their name, otherwise you could be so busy shaking hands and trying to make a good impression that you don't even register their name, let alone remember it. Next, immediately associate the face and name with a mental image, the more exaggerated and extreme the better so that it will also include an emotional component (e.g. if the image is funny, scary, cute, etc.).

2. Someone introduces himself as Simon Campbell, so you might imagine him taking a bath in a huge tin of Campbell's tomato soup with Simon Cowell, or selling pies (Simon pie man) by ringing a bell. Involve as many senses as possible in your little scenario, to relate information to colours, textures, smells and tastes. Smell the soup, taste the pies, feel the texture of the flaky pie pastry in your mouth.

3. Study the person's face, take one of their memorable features and exaggerate it so that it forms part of the crazy scene. If Simon has a big nose, imagine this huge conk getting tangled up in Simon Cowell's chest hair, or stirring the soup.

4. Try to use the name once or twice during your conversation, even if it's only to say goodbye. Don't keep repeating the name because it will be obvious that you are either being insincere or that you've just read a book about memory techniques.

5. After the conversation has ended, spend half a minute consolidating the name with the mental image and then review all the names you want to remember a few hours later when you have a quiet moment to yourself.

6. Link the name to a place. Even recalling where you met will trigger other associations and aid your recall. Alternatively you can mentally transport the person to a place that is linked to their name, so it might be your friend Simon's house, or a tent on a campsite (Campbell).

ENJOYABLE AMBIGUITY, PARADOXES AND
OPTICAL ILLUSIONS

The romantic poet John Keats only once mentioned one of his core ideas about creativity, which he called 'negative capability'. In a letter to his brother dated Sunday, 21 December 1817, Keats wrote, 'at once it struck me, what quality went to form a Man of Achievement especially in literature & which Shakespeare possessed so enormously – I mean Negative Capability, that is when man is capable of being in uncertainties, Mysteries, doubts without any irritable reaching after fact & reason'.

According to Dr David Rock, author of *Your Brain at Work: Strategies for Overcoming Distraction, Regaining Focus, and Working Smarter All Day Long*, 'the brain is primed to experience at least a mild threat from most forms of uncertainty'. Success and creativity require discipline, structure, dedication and a clear vision, but the quality that ties these attributes together is the courage to tolerate uncertainty. Great leaders have this and so do great artists and sportspeople.

The need for certainty and control is detrimental to our creativity, as David Bayles and Ted Orland explain in their book *Art & Fear: Observations on the Perils (and Rewards) of Artmaking*: 'People who need certainty in their lives are less likely to make art that is risky, subversive, complicated, iffy, suggestive or spontaneous. What's really needed is . . . an overriding willingness to embrace mistakes and surprises . . . and tolerance for uncertainty is the prerequisite for succeeding.'

It is curious that so many of us seek the safety of certainty and yet we are thrilled and intrigued by optical illusions. We are delighted by the bafflement, the paradox of knowing that our senses are being fooled, that our perceptions are vulnerable and fragile. Expand your creativity and well-being by embracing uncertainty. Don't rush to solve a problem because, to quote the author Alexander Cheung, 'it is in ambiguity that dreams are hatched, hopes are nurtured, and possibilities run wild'.

Here are some optical illusions. Remember the wonder you experience from viewing them to remind you that uncertainty can be healthy and exhilarating; it doesn't have to be met with fear and a furrowed brow.

STRAIGHT LINES?

ACCENTUATE THE POSITIVE

1. Look at the yellow dot for 15 seconds

2. Now look here

Optical illusion cube

These concentric circles
resemble one single spiral.

The Penrose triangle

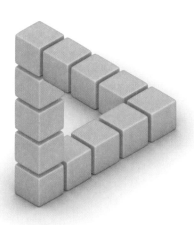

Stare at the white dot and
the picture will start to move.

BIG PICTURE THINKING

Big picture thinkers are imaginative, strategic and visionary but they can be disorganized, impulsive, easily bored and lack attention to detail. At the other end of the spectrum, the detail-conscious people work on the logistics, the nuts and bolts, the finer details that the big picture people overlook. In any organization there should be a healthy mix of both kinds of people.

Of course, most of us lie somewhere along the spectrum rather than at the edges, but we all have a preference or strength for big picture or details. However, the big picture people tend to be the leaders, the CEOs, the generators of ideas, the paradigm shifters. They create something that makes everyone else scratch their heads and say, 'Why didn't I think of that?' They can usually employ teams of detail merchants to make their vision a reality so they don't really need to sweat the small stuff. But if you're a detail monkey and you want to broaden your horizons, these strategies will help you.

To become a big picture thinker, you just have to copy what big picture thinkers do and no one saw a bigger picture than Steve Jobs.

He created a company that was totally design driven and valued beauty and human intuition above spreadsheets and quarterly reports. He didn't just think globally but even bigger! One of his famous aspirations was 'I want to put a ding in the universe'. The attention to detail of Apple design is also legendary, but it is all driven by the untiring quest for simplicity and purity. Jobs knew what people wanted. He never got so distracted by details that he forgot that customers are emotional beings. He had vaulting ambition, intuition, a desire for beauty and a relentless focus on the emotional experience of real people. You may not share Jobs's ambition but the other three motivations are what make us human and life worth living.

When you watch a film in which a corporate cog throws his papers in the air and escapes from his cubicle, it's because he or she has suddenly seen the bigger picture – people, beauty and intuition. In *The Matrix*, the exact same motivations lead Neo out of the office and down the rabbit hole where he literally sees the bigger picture.

When you look at it like that, who wouldn't want to ignore the details and become a big thinker?

BECOMING A BIG THINKER

1. Imagine the possibilities. This requires courage and some may say a big ego, but the first step to allowing yourself to think big is honesty. Be honest with yourself about what you really want and your perspective will change.

2. Follow your intuition. This doesn't mean you won't make mistakes. In fact, it will mean making more mistakes, but it will indicate that you are travelling somewhere rather than standing still. Attention to detail can also be synonymous with sticking to the comfort of what we know, getting distracted by the little stuff, instead of having the courage to take bigger risks.

3. Allow yourself to become emotionally attached to the bigger picture. This invites the possibility of getting emotionally hurt. No one ever got hurt by something they didn't care about but nothing has ever been achieved without individuals who were prepared to lay themselves on the line and to encourage the passion and commitment that creates this vulnerability.

4. Start right away doing whatever you think you need to do to make the bigger picture a reality. This involves action rather than thinking, talking or dreaming.

5. Now you can be strategic. Now you can bring focused, detailed strategy into play because it is a tool to serve the big picture rather than an emotional blinker or something you have to do because it comes with your pay level.

6. Always make your attention to detail serve the bigger goal.

KILL THE ANTS

The acronym ANTs stands for Automatic Negative Thoughts, which are a major, controllable factor in our daily experience. Learning to recognize and combat them affects our brains at a deep chemical, endocrinal level.

A recent study co-authored by Drs Andrea J. Levinson and Zafiris J. Daskalakis of the Centre for Addiction and Mental Health (CAMH) has found that people with major depressive disorders have altered functions of the neurotransmitter GABA (gamma-aminobutyric acid). In the study, people with the most treatment-resistant forms of illness had the greatest reductions of GABA levels in the brain.

Scientists agree that our brains and bodies are controlled by neurotransmitters which communicate by releasing chemicals. Our every thought and emotion involves the release of chemicals. Dr Levinson says that 'GABA provides the necessary inhibitory effect that we need in order to block out excessive brain activity that in depression may lead to excessive negative thinking.'

It is well known that the stress hormone cortisol affects learning and memory, lowers immune function and bone density, increases blood pressure and cholesterol and at increased levels can ultimately lead to heart disease. Cortisol is released in response to fear or stress by the adrenal glands as part of the fight-or-flight mechanism and after its release it remains elevated for several hours.

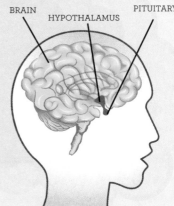

BRAIN   HYPOTHALAMUS   PITUITARY

The pituitary gland is an endocrine (hormone-producing) gland. It is about the size of a pea and is located at the base of the brain, behind the bridge of your nose. Among the many hormones it releases (including growth hormone and thyroid-stimulating hormone) the gland produces the important Adrenocorticotrophic Hormone (ACTH) which regulates levels of cortisol.

So your thoughts and emotions directly affect the chemical activity in your brain. Your thoughts do matter. Clearly an imbalance in brain chemistry cannot be cured simply by positive thinking, but it is worth noting that although you can't think and feel your way out of major depressive disorders, you do have some control over the chemical reactions that are happening in your brain.

RECOGNIZE NEGATIVE THOUGHTS

1. **Hyperbole:** in negative situations, whenever you use expressions like 'I never', 'I always' or 'that's typical' you are overgeneralizing and exaggerating the negative. Switch this around and make it a rule that you will only use hyperbole when something GOOD happens. This will reinforce a belief that good things regularly happen to you (which is true, but we are programmed to remember and pay more attention to threats and negative experiences – it's called negativity bias – a trait that kept our ancestors from being eaten by predators, but not so useful to modern humans who make far fewer daily life and death decisions).

2. **Prediction:** we ridicule those who claim to be able to predict the future, especially if they are making money from it, but we think nothing of making negative predictions about our own lives. Since no one can predict the future, it makes no sense to base our present decisions on this and even less sense to choose negative predictions over positive ones.

3. **Projection:** this is just as flawed as prediction, but happens in real time. We think we know what other people are thinking, so we act accordingly. We think a person hates us, so we avoid them; we assume someone looks down on us so we become haughty or defensive. Again, it is impossible to know another person's thoughts so it makes no sense to choose negative ones over positive.

These three ANTs – hyperbole, prediction and projection – wreak havoc with our pituitary glands. Many people avoid 'positive thinking' because it appears to be such a simplistic and reductive approach to complex human behaviour and, above all, because it seems phoney. Yet those same people allow an equally phoney negative belief system to dominate their lives. So make the ANTs work for you. You probably can't stop yourself from hyperbolic thinking, prediction and projection, but you can change the operands from negative to positive.

TRUST YOUR INTUITION

In a recent article in *Seed* magazine called 'Who Wants to be a Cognitive Neuroscience Millionaire?', Ogi Ogas, a final-year PhD student at Boston University's doctoral programme in cognitive neuroscience, explains how his understanding of the human brain helped him to win $500,000 on the *Who Wants to be a Millionaire?* game show. He explicitly links intuition with memory and begins his analysis by stating, 'Folk wisdom holds that on standardized tests you should go with your first impulse. Research tends to support this idea: a first impulse is more often correct than a second, revised decision.'

Visual closure is the ability to visualize a complete whole from incomplete information or a partial picture (*see* page 107). A similar process, called priming, occurs with memory which Ogi Ogas says was his first technique: 'The priming of a memory occurs because of the peculiar "connectionist" neural dynamics of our cortex, where memories are distributed across many regions and neurons. If we can recall any fragment of a pattern, our brains tend to automatically fill in the rest.' He used priming to answer the $16,000 question: 'This past spring, which country first published inflammatory cartoons of the prophet Muhammad?' He didn't know the answer, but he remembered having a conversation with his friend Gena about it, so he chatted with the host Meredith Vieira about this conversation and tried to recall where and when it took place and whatever details he could remember. Suddenly he pictured Gena rolling his eyes and saying, 'What else would you expect from Denmark?'

However, he says that he used 'pure intuition' to correctly answer the $250,000 question: 'The department store Sears got its start by selling what specific product in its first catalogue?' Once again, he didn't know the answer but the word 'watches' popped into his head before the answers were displayed and he also thought of railroads. When he got home he looked up the details and discovered that railroad station agent Richard Sears had sold watches to other station agents along the Minneapolis and St. Louis Railway for a year before meeting up with Alvah C. Roebuck. At some point in the past he must have been exposed to this information and his intuition retrieved part of that memory. His intuition didn't just come out of the ether; it was the result of buried memories.

Here are ten general knowledge questions. If you don't know the answers, that's a bonus. Write down the thoughts that spring to mind, like Ogi Ogas's 'watches'. Tune into all the 'I-was-going-to-say-that' thoughts and make a note of them. Then see where these key words lead you as you dredge your memory. Finally, check the answers on page 144 and look up some further details on Wikipedia and see if you can find a connection between your intuition and the actual facts. There will be some instances that prove that your intuition was actually linked to a distant memory.

1. What does HTML stand for?

2. Which nation first gave women the right to vote?

3. Who was the ancient Greek goddess of agriculture?

4. Who was La Divina?

5. Who is America's most published playwright?

6. The Chinese called this vegetable 'mad apple', believing it to cause insanity.

7. Who painted *Las Meninas*?

8. What two cities were linked by the Orient Express?

9. What is philematology?

10. What was used to erase lead pencil marks before rubber came into use?

CROSSING THE MIDLINE

Your vertical midline is an imaginary line drawn from the top of your head, along the bridge of your nose, through your navel and ending between your legs. Crossing the midline – moving a part of the body so that it operates on the other side of the line – is a vitally important skill for brain development and motor coordination in babies and young children. In fact, it is one of the developmental goals that paediatricians look for at a baby's six-month check-up.

Crossing the midline is necessary for bilateral coordination ('ability to use both sides of the body at the same time') and dominance in one hand, which is important for fine motor skills such as writing. Typically, children with low muscle tone lack the requisite core stability to twist their bodies to cross the midline, so both bilateral coordination and hand dominance will be delayed along with other cognitive skills such as reading (which is a crossing the midline activity). Children who have difficulty crossing the midline may appear ambidextrous, which should be a cause for concern, not a sign that the child is going to be a Premier League footballer.

CORPUS CALLOSUM

The right side of the brain controls the left side of the body and the left side of the brain controls the right side of the body. The two hemispheres are connected by the corpus callosum, the largest white matter structure in the brain.

Crossing the midline requires both sides working together and increases the communication between the two hemispheres. Even in adulthood, physical activities that cross the midline give your brain a complete workout and improve coordination, balance, reasoning skills, mathematical ability and creativity.

BOUNCE, CLAP, CROSS

Sit in a chair with your feet flat on the ground, your back straight (rather than slumped) and your knees facing forward (rather than splayed out wide). Hold a ball in your right hand. To a count of four, bounce it onto the floor between your legs (1), catch it with your left hand (2), pass the ball to your right hand (3) and then bend your elbow so that both hands come to rest at shoulder height (4), ready to begin the sequence again. Repeat for three minutes. For a greater challenge you can increase the speed, but make sure you don't lose the rhythm.

HEEL TAP

Stand with your legs shoulder width apart with your arms by your side. To a count of eight:

1. With your weight on your left leg, bend your right knee and bring your right heel across the midline until you can touch it with your left hand (keep your left hand on your left side, rather than move it right to meet your foot).

2. Return your right foot to its starting position.

3. With your weight on your right leg, bend your left knee and bring your left heel across the midline until you can touch it with your right hand (keep your right hand on your right side, rather than move it left to meet your foot).

4. Return your left foot to its starting position.

5. Repeat steps 1–4, only this time move each leg behind the other leg.

ELBOW TAP

Stand with your legs shoulder width apart with your arms by your side. To a count of four, bend and touch right elbow to left knee as you raise your leg, stand and then touch left elbow to right knee.

GRAPEVINE WALKING

Stand facing forward with your legs together and arms by your side.

1. Take five steps to the right (step your left leg in front of your right leg, then move your right leg to the right, while continuing to face forward).

2 Take five steps to the left (step your right leg in front of your left leg, then move your left leg to the left, while continuing to face forward).

3. Repeat steps 1–2, moving your leading foot behind the standing leg.

REVERSE
BRAINSTORMING

Sometimes we have to stand on our head to change our perspective and solve a problem. Reverse brainstorming is just like regular brainstorming only instead of trying to find a solution to a problem, the aim is to find all the ways that you could *cause* the problem or make it worse.

Instead of asking 'How can I succeed in this endeavour' you explore ways that you can really mess it up and then take those suggestions and reverse them again to reach a solution.

This process will highlight assumptions and weaknesses and may be a revelation, since you may discover that some of the strategies that you thought were helping to solve the problem might actually be contributing to it.

QUESTION: HOW CAN WE ATTRACT MORE CUSTOMERS TO SPEND MONEY ON OUR ONLINE STORE?

Reverse the question: How can we ensure that **fewer** customers spend money on our online store?

Brainstorm for as many ideas as possible . . .

- Make sure meta description is full of irrelevant and misleading details, or have hundreds of them with spammy repeats and put them in the wrong location
- Remove cross-linking between pages on the website
- Lower our search engine ranking
- Increase our prices
- Make the website hard to navigate and boring to look at
- Reduce quality of goods
- Display poor customer feedback prominently on the home page
- Never update the website
- Have lots of broken links
- Have poor spelling and grammar
- Copy and paste sales material from other websites

- Break off trading links with other websites
- Link with websites that have nothing to do with ours
- Avoid social media

Now reverse again . . .

- Check meta tags are accurate; stick to one keyword phrase per page; name each page; read an article about effective Google searches for tips on how to optimize our website
- Find out whether meta tags are even important any more
- Improve our search engine ranking
- Check prices regularly to ensure that they are competitive
- Make the website content easy to navigate and visually stunning
- Increase quality of goods; establish an atmosphere of trust, teamwork and cooperation with suppliers; iron out any misunderstandings; ensure quality tracking is accurate
- Display glowing customer feedback prominently on the home page; deal with dissatisfied customers quickly and effectively to maintain good word-of-mouth reputation
- Constantly update the website
- Regularly check that links are active and relevant; use hyperlink names rather than 'click here'; build/add a handful of rich anchor text links each month
- Hire a proofreader?
- Make sure copy is original and customer–focused
- Increase trading links with other websites; establish linking agreements so links, deep links and framing are appropriate
- Build up our profiles; create powerful profiles on Facebook, Twitter and Google Plus

REVERSE BRAIN DUMPS

When you are searching for inspiration, open up a Word document and write down everything that comes to mind about the topic. Don't self-censor. Approach it with an open mind and a spirit of non-judgement. Include queries that need answering, emotional responses (likes and dislikes, hopes and fears, etc.) and allow your intuition to prime your memory to produce deep associations. Now look at what you've created and reverse it – reverse queries and questions, write down the antonyms to everything you've come up with and see where they take you.

ROUTINE-BREAKING

It is well established that novelty is good for the brain and body, increases your alertness, attention and creativity and makes your brain form new neural connections. The best way to keep your brain youthful is to present it with new stimulation, to break your routines and give your brain what it craves the most: a break from the norm.

Have you noticed how exhausting foreign holidays are? Aside from the travelling, change in climate, increase in physical activity and overindulgence in food and drink, one of the main reasons is that your brain is working much harder; it is bombarded with new experiences, novel sights, sounds, smells, tastes, textures, colours, the challenges of a foreign language, unfamiliar customs and social observances. All this rich new input is, however, very good for your brain and your creative juices.

New experiences encourage the growth of dendrites, the branched projections which receive electrochemical messages from other neurons. The more your dendrites develop and branch out, the greater the surface area available for receiving information, so the more complex the electrochemical stimulation received from other neural cells.

You don't have to go on holiday to mix things up and break your routine. Here are some routine-breaking suggestions to fertilize your dendrites:

1. Take a shower with your eyes closed. Your other senses will become heightened, the smells of the shower gel and shampoo, the tingle of the water on your skin, the steam in your nostrils, the water in your ears and sloshing around your toes. Your spatial awareness will also be challenged as you fumble for objects.

2. Use your non-dominant hand or foot to perform everyday tasks like brushing your teeth, scooping an omelette out of the pan, opening a door, using keys, washing, holding a knife and fork, drinking, walking the dog, etc.

3. Step outside your comfort zone. Challenge yourself to do one thing a week that scares you (without intentionally exposing yourself to physical danger).

4. Choose some music you think you will really hate and really pay attention to the musical structures, the tropes and the clichés, but also try to bridge the gap between you and the music to allow the possibility that you could enjoy it; after all, somebody bothered to create it and it's been released, so someone must think it's worth a listen.

5. The next time you go to a coffee shop or a restaurant, choose something on the menu that you would normally overlook.

6. Take risks. Those who risk nothing, gain nothing.

7. Ask someone who you know has a different taste in literature to recommend one of their favourite books. Read it. No matter that you like spy thrillers and your friend just loves chick lit. Give it a chance. At the very least, it gives you another point of common connection with your buddy.

8. Start saying yes and no more often. Say yes to the stuff that you know you ought to say yes to but are too frightened to explore; say no more often to social engagements and commitments that are over-extending you and which you are only doing out of a sense of duty.

9. Talk to people you wouldn't normally talk to.

10. Every week perform one spontaneous and no-strings-attached act of kindness.

BIBLIOGRAPHY

HOW TO DEAL WITH INTRUSIVE THOUGHTS

1. Wegner, Daniel. *White Bears and Other Unwanted Thoughts: An Exploration of Suppression, Obsession, and the Psychology of Mental Control*. New York: Viking, 1989.

2. Israel, Richard and North, Vanda. *Mind Chi: Re-wire Your Brain in 8 Minutes a Day, Strategies for Success in Business and Life*. Capstone, 2010.

AWAKEN YOUR SENSES

1. Nittono, H., Fukushima, M., Yano, A., & Moriya, H. 'The Power of Kawaii: Viewing Cute Images Promotes a Careful Behavior and Narrows Attentional Focus.' *PLoS ONE*, September 26, 2012.

2. Sanders M. A., Shirk, S. D., Burgin, C. J., Martin, L. L. 'The Gargle Effect: Rinsing the Mouth With Glucose Enhances Self-Control.' Psychological Science, 2012.

DIGITAL DISTRACTIONS

Rosen, Larry. *iDisorder: Understanding Our Obsession with Technology and Overcoming Its Hold on Us*. New York: Palgrave Macmillan, 2012.

THE 'FIVE MORE' RULE

Walton, Greg and Dweck, Carol. 'Willpower: It's in Your Head.' *New York Times*, November 26, 2011.

SOLUTION-FOCUSED THINKING

Beck, Aaron. 'Self-Focus in Cognitive Therapy', Beck Institute. YouTube, September 4, 2013.

LATERAL THINKING

de Bono, Edward. *The Use of Lateral Thinking*. London: Jonathan Cape, 1967.

PARALLEL THINKING

de Bono, Edward. *Six Thinking Hats*. London: Little Brown and Company, 1985.

VERBAL REASONING

Flower, Sydney B. Brinkle, John R. *The Goat-gland Transplantation, As Originated and Successfully Performed by J. R. Brinkley, M. D., of Milford, Kansas, U. S. A., in Over 600 Operations Upon Men and Women*. Chicago: New Thought Book Department, 1921. Released by The Project Gutenberg, EBook #29362, July 2009.

SPOT THE RELATIONSHIP BETWEEN NUMBERS

Du Sautoy, Marcus. *The Number Mysteries: A Mathematical Odyssey Through Everyday Life*. London: Fourth Estate, 2010.

PRIME NUMBERS AND THE HUMAN BRAIN

Bershadskii, A. 'Hidden Periodicity and Chaos in the Sequence of Prime Numbers.' *Advances in Mathematical Physics*, 2011.

ALGORITHMS AND ARTIFICIAL INTELLIGENCE

Wolchover, Natalie. 'As Machines Get Smarter, Evidence They Learn Like Us.' *Quanta Magazine*, July 23, 2013.

VISUAL DISCRIMINATION

Sachs, Oliver. *The Man Who Mistook His Wife for a Hat*. London: Duckworth, 1985.

VISUAL MEMORY

http://www.stephenwiltshire.co.uk/press_releases/
March_2011.pdf, The Stephen Wiltshire Gallery Ltd,
2011.

ACROSTICS

Godwin, Francis. *Rerum Anglicarum Henrico VIII,
Eduardo VI, et Maria Regnantibus, Annales.* London:
John Bill, 1616.

MULTISENSORY INPUT

Dihn, H. Q., Walker, N., Hodges, L. F., Song, C.,
Kobayashi, A. 'Evaluating the Importance of
Multisensory Input on Memory and the Sense of
Presence in Virtual Environments.' *Proceedings of the
IEEE Virtual Reality 1999*, 1999.

**ENJOYABLE AMBIGUITY, PARADOXES AND
OPTICAL ILLUSIONS**

1. Rock, David. *Strategies for Overcoming Distraction,
   Regaining Focus, and Working Smarter All Day Long.*
   New York: HarperCollins, 2009.

2. Bayles, David and Orland, Ted. *Art & Fear:
   Observations on the Perils (and Rewards) of
   Artmaking.* Santa Barbara, California: Capra Press,
   1993.

3. Cheung, Alexander. '10 Ways of Approaching Life to
   Help Anyone Embrace Ambiguity.'
   Alexanderous (blog), March 28, 2013.

KILL THE ANTS

1. Levinson A. J., Fitzgerald P. B., Favalli G., Blumberger
   D.M., Daigle M., Daskalakis Z.J. 'Evidence of Cortical
   Inhibitory Deficits in Major Depressive Disorder.'
   Biological Psychiatry, March 2010.

2. Centre for Addiction and Mental Health. 'Critical
   Brain Chemical Shown to Play Role in Severe
   Depression.' *ScienceDaily*, March 6, 2010.

TRUST YOUR INTUITION

Ogas, Ogi. 'Who Wants to be a Cognitive
Neuroscience Millionaire?' *Seed Magazine*, March
2014.

ANSWERS

P9: INCREASE PRODUCTIVITY

Barrel of beer: Tilt the barrel until the beer touches the lip. If any of the bottom of the barrel is visible, it is less than half full.

Three light bulbs: Press the first switch, leave for one minute and then turn off. Press the second switch, then enter the room. The illuminated bulb is switch 2, the warm bulb is switch 1 and the cold bulb is switch 3.

Good Samaritan: Choose the old lady. Ask your friend to drive her in your car to the hospital, so you can wait at the bus stop with your perfect partner.

P11: ATTENTIONAL CONTROL

Count the squares: 40

How many Fs?: 6, 9, 6

P13: HOW TO DEAL WITH INTRUSIVE THOUGHTS

Remove earworms: Jennifer Aniston, Eric Clapton, Cameron Diaz, Robert De Niro, Albert Einstein, David Letterman, Wolfgang Amadeus Mozart, Marie Osmond, Julia Roberts, Arnold Schwarzenegger, Serena Williams, Miley Cyrus

P27: SOLUTION-FOCUSED THINKING

Digital dilemma:

12 + 3 - 4 + 5 + 67 + 8 + 9 = 100

P30: DEDUCTIVE REASONING

Barbara: All penguins have beaks.

Celarent: No penguins have teeth.

Darii: Some pets have feathers.

Ferio: Some animals are not dogs.

Cesare: No hotel is a horse.

Camestres: No carrots are horses.

Festino: Some women are not bald.

Baroco: Some pink things are not carrots.

Darapti: Some tasty things are nutritious.

Disamis: Some delicate things are colourful.

Datisi: Some endangered things are agile.

Felapton: Some of the yellow items in this bowl are not fresh. (There may be items in the bowl other than fruit.)

Bocardo: Some animals have no tails.

Ferison: Some green things have no wheels.

Bramantip: Some ostentatious clothing is in my wardrobe.

Camenes: No flowers grown indoors are coloured.

Dimaris: Some friendly dogs are big.

Fesapo: Some neighbourly people are not Hollywood actors.

Fresison: Some evil creatures are not pandas.

P35: INDUCTIVE REASONING

Which comes next in the series?

Question 1

Rule 1: The square moves from bottom right to middle to top left. This sequence then repeats.

Rule 2: The circle moves 3 squares anticlockwise around the edge of the grid.

Answer: D

Question 2

Rule 1: The triangle pointing upwards follows the sequence top left, bottom right, bottom left, top right. This sequence then repeats.

Rule 2: The triangle pointing downwards follows the sequence top right, bottom left, bottom right. This sequence then repeats.

Answer: E

Question 3

Rule 1: The number of dots predicts how many triangles there will be in the next box.

Rule 2: The triangles are red if the number of triangles is even, blue if the number of triangles is odd.

Answer: A

Question 4

Rule 1: The shapes move one corner clockwise each time.

Rule 2: The shapes alternate between square and circle.

Rule 3: The shading changes between shaded and unshaded every other step. i.e. shaded, shaded, unshaded, unshaded, shaded, shaded, etc.

Answer: E

Question 5

Rule 1: The shapes shrink from large, medium to small, then start again.

Rule 2: The shapes alternate between triangle and circle.

Rule 3: The colours go white, to red, to blue and then repeat.

Answer: D

Question 6

Rule 1: The shape is rotated 45 degrees clockwise.

Rule 2: The shape loses a line and then an arrow each time.

Rule 3: A circle is always purple unless an arrow is pointing at it.

Answer: E

Question 7

Rule 1: The face changes in sequence from smiley to ambivalent to sad.

Rule 2: The shape alternates between square and circle.

Rule 3: The shape symbol is green for two steps then clear for two steps.

Rule 4: The shapes move one corner clockwise each turn.

Answer: D

Question 8

Rule 1: The square appears every third step.

Rule 2: The triangle alternates between rotating clockwise 90 degrees around the middle of the square and being mirrored vertically.

Rule 3: The circle alternates between being present and absent.

Answer: A

Question 9

Rule 1: If the number of purple dots is greater than the number of red dots, subtract a purple dot.

Rule 2: If the number of purple dots is smaller or equal to the number of red dots, add two purple dots.

Rule 3: Add a red dot each step.

Answer: D

P39: ABDUCTIVE REASONING

Base rate fallacy: 1a, 2b

Prosecutor's fallacy: c

P42: BOOLEAN LOGIC

1. As one of them is lying and one of them is telling the truth, Bonnie must be lying. So Clyde is telling the truth, and Bonnie stole it.

2. John is a liar and his wife tells the truth. They can't both be liars, because if John was a liar he can't make a truthful statement. If only his wife is a liar, then John would be lying about himself being truthful.

3. Pick from the one labelled 'NUTS AND BOLTS'. Since it is wrongly labelled, it must contain either only nuts or only bolts. Once you've labelled this box correctly, you can deduce the other two (e.g. if you pick a bolt, then the box labelled NUTS must be NUTS AND BOLTS since it can't be NUTS or BOLTS; if you pick a nut, then the box labelled BOLTS must be NUTS AND BOLTS since it can't be either BOLTS or NUTS).

P45: GEOMETRIC REASONING

1.

2.

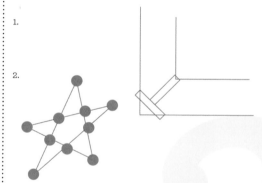

3. A square manhole cover can be dropped diagonally through the hole, while a circular one cannot.

4. White. It was a polar bear and the hunter's camp was at the North Pole.

5. 15.92cm. The radius of a circle is always approximately 1/6.28 (or 0.1592) of its circumference, so increasing the circumference of any circle by 1 metre increases the radius of that circle by (0.1592 x 100 cm) = 15.92 cm.

6.

7. The pizza is rectangular. Make two horizontal and three vertical cuts.

P47: SPATIAL THINKING
1. C, A, D
2. A
   C and E
   D
   D
   B
   B
   E

P52: LATERAL THINKING
1. There is no soil in a hole.
2. Eight
3. John

P53: LATERAL THINKING CONTINUED
1. Window
2. During a forest fire, a fire-fighting plane had scooped water from the lake, including a swimmer.
3. He lives in a houseboat in the middle of the ocean.
4. The baby fell from a ground-floor window.
5. He asked each builder to name the best builder other than themselves. He then employed the one with the most recommendations.
6. The glass was empty.
7. He was walking.
8. He was in a balloon with several other passengers; it was losing height and about to crash so they drew lots; he drew the broken match and jumped to save the others.
9. The last person took the basket with the last egg still inside.
10. The poison was in the ice cubes, which hadn't melted when he had his drink.
11. The Archduke Ferdinand was sewn into his uniform so that he looked smart, but it could not be removed.
12. The room is the ballroom of an ocean liner. The man ran out of air while diving in the wreck.
13. Police uniform; Tommy had been kept all his life in the cellar.
14. The woman had already put sugar into her tea.
15. The date reads the same upside down; will next happen in 6009.
16. He had just visited his wife who was on a life-support machine in the hospital. As he walked down the stairs the lights went out, indicating a power cut.
17. Exactly twice the distance from one end to the middle.
18. The rest of the poker players were women.
19. She was a woman driving in Saudi Arabia.
20. If it is someone she likes she can say she has just arrived; if it is someone she doesn't like she can pretend she is about to go out.
21. Sister.
22. You don't bury survivors.
23. At least one with any certainty.
24. The man had jumped from a plane but his parachute had failed. It was the unopened package.
25. She was a circus tight-rope walker who walked blindfolded over a high wire. The band used to stop playing to tell her when she had reached safety at the other end, but a stand-in conductor didn't know this and stopped the music too early. She stepped off the wire to her death.
26. The man had hiccups.
27. The taxi driver had heard his original instructions at the beginning of the journey.
28. The first tattoo artist must have done the superior eagle tattoo since it was on the other tattoo artist's back.

P58: SIMPLE SOLUTIONS ARE BEST
The seven bridges of Königsberg: no, it is impossible
Five room puzzle:

Only if he walks through corners.
Four forward-thinking camels: first a camel from one side moves forward; then two camels from the other side move forward, then three camels from the other side, etc.

1. Throw it vertically into the air.
2. The words rhyme with 1, 2, 3, etc.
3. Copernican revolution: 16, the number of dots around a centre dot.

P62: VERBAL REASONING

Make no assumptions

1. pushover, rugby; maiden, duck; drizzle, precipitate
2. cheese, slow, kick
3. classification
4. soporific, soothing
5. tribulation, contentment
6. marsh, swamp
7. aerobatics
8. car = carton, scarab, vicars, trocar
9. t
10. t, p; z, r
11. m, s, a; a, a, i
12. 1 true; 2 cannot say; 3 false; 4 true; 5 cannot say; 6 cannot say; 7 cannot say; 8 false; 9 cannot say; 10 cannot say

P68: THE HUMAN SPELLCHECKER

On opening the little door, two hairy monsters flew at my throat, bearing me down, and extinguishing the light; while a mingled guffaw **from Heathcliff** and Hareton put the copestone on my rage and **humiliation**. Fortunately, the **beasts** seemed more bent on stretching **their** paws, and yawning, and flourishing their tails, **than** devouring me alive; but they would suffer no **resurrection**, and I was forced to lie till their malignant masters pleased to deliver me: then, hatless and trembling with wrath, I ordered the miscreants to let me out – on their peril to keep **me** one minute longer – with several incoherent threats of retaliation that, in their indefinite depth of virulency, smacked of King Lear.

The vehemence of my agitation brought on a copious bleeding at the nose, and still Heathcliff laughed, and still I **scolded**. I don't know what would have concluded the scene, had **there** not been one person at hand rather more rational **than** myself, and more benevolent than my entertainer. This was Zillah, the stout housewife; who at length issued **forth** to inquire into **the** nature of the uproar. She **thought** that some of them had been **laying** violent hands on me; and, not daring to attack her master, she turned her vocal artillery against the younger scoundrel.

P71: VOCABULARY

argand, lerret, testiculate, exultion, flunge, scrutable, tribution, perchery

Wordsearch:

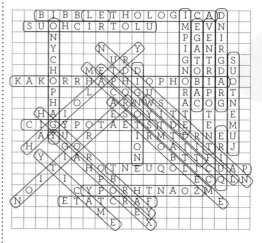

Word deduction:

abacinate	to blind using a red-hot metal plate
balaniferous	acorn-bearing
caducity	being of a transitory or impermanent nature
decastich	ten-line poem
eclogue	pastoral or rustic poem
fabulist	one who invents fables
ganoid	having shiny smooth scales
habilable	capable of being clothed
ignify	to burn
janitrix	a female janitor
keloid	hard scar tissue which grows over injured skin
landau	horse-drawn carriage with folding top
macrotous	big-eared
naevus	birthmark
octad	set of eight things
palpebration	winking
quadrilocular	having four compartments
ranivorous	frog-eating
sanative	healing
tardiloquous	slow in speech
unguligrade	walking on hoofs
vaticide	killing of a prophet
widgeon	freshwater duck
xanthic	yellowish

| yelm | a straight bundle of straw used for thatching |
| zymosis | process of infection |

P76: RIDDLES

The Riddle of the Sphinx: Man, who crawls on all fours as a baby, walks on two feet as an adult and uses a walking stick in old age.

Einstein's riddle: The German

Twelve riddles

1. If Zeheratzade doesn't know the answer, that must mean that Soraya and Peri-banu are wearing different coloured hats; so now Soraya knows what colour hat she's wearing because it must be a different colour to Peri-banu's.
2. two
3. footsteps
4. an umbrella
5. a snail
6. a chick in an egg
7. The four men were pall-bearers; the other stayed dry inside the coffin
8. a cloud
9. a candle
10. the letter R
11. a nail in a horseshoe
12. the moon

Dingbats: back draft, all around the world, paradox, right under your nose, look both ways, scrambled eggs, overwhelming odds, goatee, three square meals, West Indies, counting on you, up in arms.

P81: ALGEBRA AND THE VANISHING CAMEL

pumpkin = 30, alarm clock = 20, ice lolly = 6
car = 9, gift box = 1, guitar = 29
He added his camel to the herd. He then led nine camels (one half of 18) to the eldest son, six camels (one third of 18) to the middle son and two camels (one ninth of 18) to the youngest son. That just left his own camel, which he promptly mounted and rode away. The mathematician solved the problem by recognizing that the sum of 1/2, 1/3 and 1/9 is not 1, but 17/18. Adding an extra camel made the division possible because 18 is the lowest common denominator of 2, 3 and 9 and so 9/18 + 6/18 + 2/18 = 17/18.

P83: NUMBER SEQUENCES

1. 233 = 1, 1, 2, 3, 5, 8, 13, 21, 34, 55, 89, 144, 233
2. a) 64, 81 (square numbers series $1^2, 2^2, 3^2 \ldots 8^2, 9^2$)

   b) 21, 28 (add a row each time to make a bigger triangle)
   c) 51, 70
   d) 3125, 46656 ($1^1, 2^2, 3^3, 4^4, 5^5, 6^6 \ldots$)
3. It is alphabetical:
   eight; four; four; nine; nine; seven; six; three; three; two; zero

P88: SPOT THE RELATIONSHIP BETWEEN NUMBERS

1.

Blue	7	14	21	28
35	42	49	**56**	63
70	77	84	91	98

Red	12	**24**	36	**48**
60	**72**	84	**96**	

Yellow	13	26	39	52
65	78	91		

Predator	8	16	**24**	32
40	**48**	**56**	64	**72**
80	88	**96**		

a) red
b) blue
c) yellow

2. Here is the grid with the 25 prime numbers highlighted. The sequence 4, 4, 2, 2, 3, 2, 2, 3, 2, 1 refers to the number of primes in each row (going from top to bottom) and 5, 1, 7, 0, 1, 0, 6, 0, 5, 0 refers to the number of primes in each column (going from left to right).

1	2	3	4	5	6	7	8	9	10
11	12	13	14	15	16	17	18	19	20
21	22	23	24	25	26	27	28	29	30
31	32	33	34	35	36	37	38	39	40
41	42	43	44	45	46	47	48	49	50
51	52	53	54	55	56	57	58	59	60
61	62	63	64	65	66	67	68	69	70
71	72	73	74	75	76	77	78	79	80
81	82	83	84	85	86	87	88	89	90
91	92	93	94	95	96	97	98	99	100

3. 2584/1597 = phi

P91: PRIME NUMBERS AND THE HUMAN BRAIN

1. 13, 29, 53
2. He proved that the set of prime numbers is infinite
3. 15,485,863 is the one-millionth prime

P96: VISUAL DISCRIMINATION

1. Spot the difference
   1. Lady's red swimming costume changed to olive.
   2. Yellow umbrella changed to pink.
   3. New umbrella added beside the Nestlé wind break.
   4. Swimmers in the sea have been deleted.
   5. 'Simonis' wording has been flipped.
   6. Blue tent changed to green.
   7. Shark fin added to the sea.
   8. Duplication of striped umbrella.
   9. Lady's red top has changed to purple.
   10. Duplication of boy in long green shorts.
2. Shape matching
   1 is D rotated
   2 is A flipped
   3 is E flipped
   4 is B flipped and rotated
   5 is C rotated
3. Crime scene
   1 is 1, 2 is 4, 3 is 6, 4 is 7, 5 is 9.

P98: CONTRAST DISCRIMINATION

1. They are the same. If you don't believe it, cut them out and put them beside each other – the shading on the front centre square causes this amazing illusion!
2. They are the same

P102: VISUAL MEMORY

1. two; 2. blue, pink and yellow; 3. red short-sleeved polo shirt; 4. nothing; 5. pink and green; 6. left; 7. row four; 8. Africa; 9. four; 10. green purse; 11. top right to bottom left; 12. calculator and socks; 13. screw fitting; 14. red; 15. two; 16. purple; 17. a book; 18. blue; 19. left; 20. orange.

P105: FIGURE GROUND

Hedgehog in plantpot on shelf; bell on light stand; bat bottom right of carpet; pineapple in chair cushion; bread on bookshelf; pencil horizontal on bookshelf; boot and hat on the wall in between plants; ear on the plant outside; paperclip on cushion on sofa; butterfly on the biscuit; tie on bookshelf.

1. All of them
2.

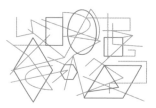

P109: VISUAL CLOSURE

Left to right: Taj Mahal, The Colosseum, Hollywood Sign, Leaning Tower of Pisa, Tower Bridge, Statue of Liberty, The Erechtheion on the Acropolis, Elizabeth Tower (Big Ben), Eiffel Tower

P113: ACROSTICS

Frances Sargent Osgood (It is a progressive acrostic: first letter of first line, second letter of the second line, third letter of the third line, etc.)
Acrostic Passwords: Stormy Monday, I Will Survive, Stand By Your Man, The Message, Stairway to Heaven, One Love, Master of Puppets, Pretty Vacant, Little Boxes, The Dock of the Bay, Can't Get You Out of My Head, We are the Champions
History of the Acrostic Puzzle: Naples, Elbe, Washington, Cincinnati, Amsterdam, Stamboul, Tornea, Lepanto, Ecliptic: NEWCASTLE, COALMINES

P130: TRUST YOUR INTUITION

1. Hyper Text Markup Language
2. New Zealand
3. Demeter
4. Maria Callas
5. Neil Simon
6. Aubergine
7. Diego Velázquez
8. Paris and Istanbul
9. The science of kissing
10. Pieces of bread